T0323504

The Lazy Winning Project Manager

Fully updated to reflect developments in artificial intelligence (AI), remote working and more, this book brings together two well-loved titles to address emerging trends and challenges in project management and personal development, offering a unique and comprehensive reference book for a new generation of project professionals.

In the ever-evolving world of project management, *The Lazy Project Manager* has been a guiding light for those seeking efficiency through unconventional strategies as well as honesty and a whole lot of fun. With *The Lazy Winner*, Peter Taylor brought his straightforward and humorous approach to personal productivity and success. Now, Peter has combined these two books to ensure a comprehensive guide for professionals seeking both project management excellence and personal fulfilment – the goal of a great work/life balance. But this book goes beyond evergreen principles, adding rich content on:

- The effectiveness of the productive lazy approach in harnessing the power of AI, demonstrating that project managers and individuals alike can leverage this hot technology
- Ways to manage projects remotely and strategies for individuals to thrive in virtual work environments, all using the productive lazy approach
- New and updated case studies showcasing how the productive lazy approach has been successfully implemented in project management scenarios and personal development journeys
- The preferences and strengths of the new generations within the workforce, and how the productive lazy approach aligns with their expectations and workstyles

Project management professionals worldwide, from new starters learning the ropes to seasoned pros looking for fresh inspiration, will welcome the latest insights and tested strategies from a project management legend.

Peter Taylor is a keynote speaker and coach and the author of the number one best-selling project management book *The Lazy Project Manager*, along with many other books. He has built and led some of the largest project teams in the world with organisations such as Siemens, IBM, UKG and now Dayforce, where he is the VP Global PMO. He has also delivered over 500 lectures around the world in 26 countries and has been described as 'perhaps the most entertaining and inspiring speaker in the project management world today'.

The Lazy Winning Project Manager

Embracing Project and Personal Productivity in an AI Empowered World

Peter Taylor

Routledge
Taylor & Francis Group

NEW YORK AND LONDON

Designed cover image: © Getty

First published 2025
by Routledge
605 Third Avenue, New York, NY 10158

and by Routledge
4 Park Square, Milton Park, Abingdon, Oxon, OX14 4RN

*Routledge is an imprint of the Taylor & Francis Group, an informa
business*

© 2025 Peter Taylor

Library of Congress Cataloging-in-Publication Data
Names: Taylor, Peter, 1957- author.
Title: The lazy winning project manage : embracing project and
personal productivity in an AI empowered world / Peter Taylor.
Description: New York, NY : Routledge, 2025. | Includes
bibliographical references and index. |
Identifiers: LCCN 2024032282 (print) | LCCN 2024032283
(ebook) | ISBN 9781032828275 (hardback) | ISBN 9781032826684
(paperback) | ISBN 9781003506522 (ebook)
Subjects: LCSH: Project management.
Classification: LCC HD69.P75 T39524 2025 (print) | LCC HD69.
P75 (ebook) | DDC 658.4/04--dc23/eng/20240802
LC record available at https://lccn.loc.gov/2024032282
LC ebook record available at https://lccn.loc.gov/2024032283

ISBN: 978-1-032-82827-5 (hbk)
ISBN: 978-1-032-82668-4 (pbk)
ISBN: 978-1-003-50652-2 (ebk)

DOI: 10.4324/9781003506522

Typeset in Times New Roman
by SPi Technologies India Pvt Ltd (Straive)

To all the people who have inspired me in the past 15 years since I first had the idea and the original book was written and published.

DAS – well on his way to some form of retirement after working me in six companies over a 30-year plus period – he has finally had enough but was generous enough to write the foreword to this book. As mentioned in the dedication in the original book, my manager, and my mentor, to which I would now add, my friend (who has never taken me to Iceland, but that is a whole different story and won't spoil our relationship excessively).

Richard Burton – as the man who apparently had nothing better to do on the day my book proposal landed on his desk and commissioned the very first book by me. Published through his company Infinite Ideas, the rest is ongoing history.

Meredith Norwich – as Senior Editor at Routledge, thank you for so taking on the beast that is the 'Lazy PM' so enthusiastically.

Juliet – my wife, who constantly teases me with "So, you're the Lazy Project Manager...", thank you for the grounding with love.

And to anyone else who knows me and cares.

Peter

Contents

CHAPTER 42
The Ultimate Question (and Answer)   **208**

Acknowledgements

Never say never again (so they say). Well, this is perhaps a classic example of why you shouldn't say 'never again'.

No sooner had I wrapped up my last book *Projects: Methods: Outcomes: The New PMO Model for True Project and Change Success*[1], in which I boldly stated that this would probably be my last project management book, than an opportunity arose to update my 'flagship'[2] creation *The Lazy Project Manager*[3].

Well, how could I refuse to wrap up this amazing journey with a revamp and an update of what has become known as a bit of a classic in my genre of writing.

Therefore, welcome once more to the world of 'Productive Laziness' – a world that will help you focus on what really matters and to remain in control, even when your project threatens to run away from you.

> "Progress isn't made by early risers. It's made by lazy people trying to find easier ways to do something"[4]
>
> Robert Heinlein[5]

Notes

1 Published December 2023 by Routledge and selling very well, thank you kindly.
2 Not my words but my publisher's.
3 Infinite Ideas Limited; First Edition (28 April 2010) and Infinite Ideas; 2nd edition (26 October 2015).
4 From *Time Enough for Love*, Robert Heinlein, US science fiction author (1907–88).

  Note: This is the quote that triggered the 'productively lazy' concept for me. Having trained many people over time in various jobs and roles, I was constantly trying to explain how it was that I, and others, seemed to be so much more relaxed, organised and less stressed than others and yet delivered similar or better results. Reading Heinlein's quote made it all seem so much clearer and simpler – I was 'lazy', and this was a good thing. A very good thing indeed, I believe.

5 Yes, this is a deliberate mis-quote since the original stated "Progress isn't made by early risers. It's made by lazy men trying to find easier ways to do something".

Foreword

It has been 15 years since the original *Lazy Project Manager* book was published, and it continues to be a seminal text, popular around the world with the project community and a constant fixture on the Amazon Project Management best-seller list.

This latest book from Peter Taylor combines *The Lazy Project Manager* and the *Lazy Winner* into a third edition, enhancing the content to bring it up to date and address the emerging trends in Project Management and personal development for a new generation of project professionals.

In the continually evolving world of project management, Peter's *The Lazy Project Manager* has been a guiding light for those seeking efficiency and who enjoy a healthy dose of fun at work through unconventional strategies and approaches, which was expanded with *The Lazy Winner* to include insights into personal productivity and success. Peter's focus has always been on the people, project managers managing themselves while managing a project.

Peter is a prolific writer and popular communicator on all things Project Management. He has written over 30 books on the topic, delivered over 500 lecturers in 26 countries and has been described as "perhaps the most entertaining and inspiring speaker in the project management world today".

Currently Peter is co-host on the Squid of Despair podcast, which takes a light-hearted and irreverent view on business topics with 'unscripted musings about business life, transformation and all the myriad other things that keep us awake at night'.

I have collaborated with Peter for over three decades and over that time seen the evolution of the Project Management discipline and more recently the rise of the Global Project Management Office (GPMO). The industry continues to evolve, and practitioners today have reference to many sources of best practice, most notably perhaps including the PMBok guide, now in its 7th edition, and the Prince2 methodology that now incorporate agile layers in their delivery techniques. Project Managers today have had to learn to incorporate many of these new digital techniques within their work, being more focused on data-driven decision-making. To be successful in this new reality project managers need to be agile and flexible, with more focus on collaboration, employee engagement, diversity and inclusion and outcome-based management. The world of project management has become more people-centric since the original *Lazy Project Manager* was published, less mechanistic and more change-orientated, and this is an ongoing theme in Peter's new version.

In this latest addition, Peter explores these new themes integrating project management and productivity, aligning project goals with individual success strategies addressing the needs of project professionals seeking to deliver both project excellence and derive personal fulfilment.

Peter also addresses the changing world of work and highlights how the productive lazy approach remains effective in harnessing newer technology like artificial intelligence, ensuring that project managers and individuals alike can leverage this new technology to their personal advantage.

The book also addresses other newer 'post-pandemic' themes like remote working and the preferences and strengths of the new workforce offering insights and strategies on how to thrive in virtual environments and showing how the 'lazy approach' can be aligned with the expectations and workstyles of this new generation of project managers.

The transformative nature of project management and personal development is open to a fresh perspective given the rapidly changing landscape in the Project Management world. This new edition of *The Lazy Project Manager*, incorporating an updated version of *The Lazy Winner*, offers a valuable source of reference to help professionals thrive in the dynamic landscape of the contemporary project-based workplace.

It is an exciting time for a renewed focus on Peter's productive lazy strategies that not only optimise project outcomes but also empower individuals to become lazy winners in their own lives.

David Ayling-Smith

David Ayling-Smith: An experienced executive with three decades of experience of selling, delivering and managing consultancy, support and maintenance operations in the Enterprise Software industry.

He has held various leadership positions with a track record of developing strategies that deliver profitable revenue growth and scalable business improvement. Having particular experience with acquisitions and business transformations, David (also known as DAS) is a strong communicator and people-focused executive with a history of building successful teams and coaching individual key players.

He also has had the pleasure (experience) of co-hosting the unusual podcast 'The Squid of Despair' with Peter.

Chapter 1

Introduction

We begin by exploring what an incredible profession project management is now and how this is, perhaps, the best time ever to be part of that growing global community.

We also try to answer the critical question of what the value to you is in buying/reading this book and how it varies from the previous two editions that may already be on your physical or digital bookshelf.

DOI: 10.4324/9781003506522-1

Now is an amazing time to be in project management

Uniform

In my well-known 'keynote' of productive laziness, based on my first book, I start by declaring that we have a problem in project management. We are, or we certainly were it seemed to me all those years ago, somewhat invisible.

I joke that when you go to project management parties play this game (come on, you've been to hundreds of those, haven't you?). OK, the game – find a project manager and get them to answer two questions with the first thing that comes into their head. OK, here goes:

Q1: What are you?
A1: I'm a project manager.
Q2: What do you do?
A2: I manage projects.

Result is – well, nothing, I am absolutely no better off understanding what you do than a minute ago.

Sigh.

The trouble is that if you actually try to get a more detailed answer, then it can rapidly turn into a rehash of a body of knowledge (and that will bore everyone at the party, and you will be left all alone in the kitchen contemplating your sad existence of a life).

Check out an article I did many years ago on explaining project management to an alien: www.linkedin.com/pulse/alien-project-management-peter-taylor.

At the time I was posing this question, my youngest son was at junior school, and they had a thing called 'bring a parent to school to tell the kids about their job'.

Never got invited[1].

Sigh.

DOI: 10.4324/9781003506522-2

A policemen got invited and talked about road safety and crime reporting and things like that. Quite popular.

A nurse came in and talked about cuts and bruises and first aid and things like that. Quite popular.

And who else? Oh yes, a fireman came in and talked about what to do in the event of a fire or someone was in trouble. Very popular (especially with the mums, apparently).

Now think about this. What do these folks have in common?

They have a uniform! Yes, they have an actual 'look at what I do' uniform. Respect!

Imagine if we had a project management uniform. Cape, bright underpants, capital 'P' on our chest. Wow!

Next day at work as you walked through the office people would cheer and say, 'thank goodness, it's a project manager, everything will all be OK now'.

Maybe set this as a challenge at your next team meeting. Design the project manager's uniform. It could be fun.

Community

The real point here is that visible or not (and we are certainly a lot less invisible these days I would suggest) the global community of project professionals is vast.

Forbes[2] suggests that *'The project management industry is witnessing unprecedented growth and is set to increase in demand over the next few years, with a predicted 25 million needed to fill the gap across various industries globally. Some of the most popular sectors with opportunities for project managers include technology, construction, manufacturing, and finance.*

This comes at a time when the technology sector is booming, with AI spurring the need for over 90 million new jobs. It turns out that roles requiring project management skills and capabilities such as people management, stakeholder management and engagement, budgeting, project planning, and resource management are becoming more of a necessity for most organizations'.

And the number of conferences[3], events, chapter meetings, presentations, webinars, books, articles and more is massive, with more each and every day, it seems.

So become part of this community and don't just sit inside your own organisation and see only your world. Experience the bigger world, contribute to it, and draw value from it.

It's bloody amazing!

Be part of your project world

I would urge you to consider the vast opportunity of the global world of project management and reflect on what part you want to play.

Project Manager is a verb (a doing word) and not a noun (a describing word) goes the old saying, and it is true, you cannot be passive in this profession, but you can be somewhere on a spectrum of active to hyper-active within the overall project community around the world. This is your choice, of course.

By more luck that intention, I have found myself to become something of a figure within the profession (not one of the serious leaders because a) that just isn't in my nature; b) I am happy to 'talk with the masses' and not just the elite; c) I seem to annoy some of the powers that be; and d) give me practice over just theory any day)[4].

What I would say is that none of my success (if this is the correct word to use) is unique to me. You can do the same, or similar, or better. You just have to want to have some kind of voice in this project world and get on and make your voice known, through speaking, through writing, through communities, through events, through volunteering or through just plain 'doing'[5].

Don't hold back – just go for it!

Notes

1 DAS: You will, if you have ever met Peter, know that he is really sensitive to these things.
2 www.forbes.com/sites/rachelwells/2023/11/10/25-million-project-managers-in-demand-as-median-salaries-soar-to-120k/?sh=2f2a306157a8.
3 As I am writing this I am actually in Orlando at a conference – it is 6 am, and I am enjoying a Starbucks (other coffees are available).
4 This slightly non-conformist attitude became apparent when I hosted an international conference some years ago and watched the wise and the worthy take to the stage – some of whom had never actually run a project and others who probably last ran a project 20 years ago. At this point I vowed to remain a real practitioner.
5 One of my greatest pleasures has been to facilitate nearly 100 people to get published in some way, from a quote in a book to a chapter contribution, all the way to co-authorship.

So, what's actually new?

Understandably you will want to know what the value to you is in buying/reading and investing your time in this book and how it varies from the previous two editions.

I've already read it

If you then I thank you, whole-heartedly.

I am assuming that you did not hate it, otherwise you would not be looking at this edition. Therefore you will no doubt ask an extremely important question.

'What is new' or 'What will I get out of this version over and above the original'.

Very fair question and one I will attempt to answer.

Well, here's the high-level summary of what you get that is 'new' and hopefully 'improved', as they love to say in washing powder advertisements (or capsules/pods if I attempt to move with the times).

Building on the current content of *The Lazy Project Manager*, the new 'third edition' incorporates the key elements of my work on personal productivity (based on my book *The Lazy Winner*), which results in two major outputs:

- Integration of Project Management and Personal Productivity

  - The relationship between effective project management and personal productivity is more critical than ever. In this book we explore the synergy between 'The Lazy Project Manager' and 'The Lazy Winner,' offers an integrated approach that aligns project goals with individual success strategies. This holistic perspective ensures a comprehensive guide for professionals seeking both project management excellence and personal fulfilment – the goal of a great work/life balance.

DOI: 10.4324/9781003506522-3

Over and above that kind of 'two for one' deal I will be addressing the following:

- Adapting to Technological Advancements

  - Both project management and personal productivity have been significantly impacted by technological advancements. Here I will showcase how the productive lazy approach remains effective in harnessing the power of artificial intelligence (AI), ensuring that project managers and individuals alike can leverage this 'hot' technology to their personal advantage.

- Addressing Remote Work Challenges in Both Arenas

  - The global shift towards remote virtual work has impacted both project management and personal productivity. As a result, I offer insights into managing projects remotely while also providing strategies for individuals to thrive in virtual work environments. This dual focus ensures that the productive lazy approach remains effective across various professional and personal contexts.

- Updated Case Studies and Real-world Examples

  - Real-world examples are pivotal for illustrating the practical application of productive lazy strategies. By updating the existing case studies in The Lazy Project Manager and introducing new ones, this new book showcases how the productive lazy approach has been successfully implemented in project management scenarios and personal development journeys, making them relevant to a broad audience.

- Catering to a New Generation of Professionals

  - The new book addresses the preferences and strengths of the new generation within the workforce. By incorporating insights on how the productive lazy approach aligns with the expectations and workstyles of the newer generation, the updated edition ensures that the wisdom shared, and loved by thousands, continues to resonate with a diverse and evolving audience.

OK, even I am laughing at that last pretentious part. But it is true that the book has sold in the thousands, that I have personally presented over 200 keynotes and webinars based on the book[1], and many people have said some very nice things about it over the years[2].

So welcome to the all-new, singing and dancing, *Lazy Project Manager* interpolating my work on personal productivity based on *The Lazy Winner*[3].

Enough said (I hope).

Personal productivity

Productive laziness is, at its heart, all about personal productivity (along with that of your project team of course) but there is another layer that is invaluable to understand when it comes to evolving to become a truly productively lazy project manager.

Key lessons and guidance from my work in this area is incorporated into this book for your easy reference and personal guide.

AI productivity

Artificial intelligence (AI) is impossible to ignore today, but back in 2009, when I was coming up with the concept of productive laziness, AI was, to the general public, a far-off future possibility.

But beyond most of our sight things were happening:

- Google starts to secretly build the first autonomous car
- Rajat Raina, Anand Madhavan and Andrew Ng published "Large-Scale Deep Unsupervised Learning Using Graphics Processors[4]," presenting the idea of using GPUs to train large neural networks
- IBM Watson[5] originated with the initial goal of beating a human on the iconic quiz show Jeopardy[6]! Is in development (In 2011, the question-answering computer system defeated the show's all-time (human) champion, Ken Jennings)

You can get a much deeper insight into the history of AI (and how it will impact project management, in my book *AI and the Project Manager: How the Rise of Artificial Intelligence Will Change Your World*, but my personal thoughts about this are AI is a great thing for project managers, because it will free us all up to focus on people, and, as a direct result, productivity and success will increase.

And (for fun) check out ChatGPT's[7] summary of *The Lazy Project Manager* in the appendices.

Why invest in this approach?

Well, don't listen to me – hear other people's thoughts in this area:

Stephen Hawking

Back in the 1980s, when Stephen Hawking's brain was the hottest commodity in town, he had a productivity routine that would make even the most disciplined looked somewhat surprised at.

Picture this: as the clock struck five or six, Hawking would pack up his black hole theories and head straight for the exit. No overtime for this smart man.

Hawking stated 'The problem with physics is that most of the days we don't make any major headway (on our projects). That's why you should do other stuff: listen to music, meet good friends. There's one exception to this rule: If you find a solution for a given problem, you work 24 hours a day and forget everything else. Until the problem is solved in its entirety[8].'

Bill Gates

Bill thinks you should hire lazy people. No, seriously. He famously said something along the lines of, 'I choose a lazy person to do a hard job. Because a lazy person will find an easy way to do it'.

But here's the kicker: laziness is often misunderstood. It can easily be mistaken for relaxation, a preference for personal tasks over professional ones, or simply not being an early bird. In the realm of tech culture, this misconception is rampant. The emphasis on appearing productive outweighs genuine productivity.

Hence my proposal, to avoid any confusion at all, is to use the term 'productive laziness'.

Though most individuals may not possess the genius of Stephen Hawking or the vision of Bill Gates[9], there lies a broader lesson for anyone aspiring to create value: seize the moment when the task demands it but allocate ample time outside those exigencies for indulging in music and meaningful social connections. Such non-work will power your productivity and thinking.

Notes

1 Over 500 in total on a range of topics. https://thelazyprojectmanager.com/speaking.
2 Some people have said some pretty nasty things about it as well – just check out the appendices for some insight into the world of feedback.
3 *The Lazy Winner: How to Do More with Less Effort and Succeed in Your Work and Personal Life without Rushing Around Like a Headless Chicken or Putting in 100 Hour Weeks.*
4 chrome-extension://efaidnbmnnnibpcajpcglclefindmkaj/http://robotics.stanford.edu/~ang/papers/icml09-LargeScaleUnsupervisedDeepLearningGPU.pdf.
5 IBM Watson is a computer system capable of answering questions posed in natural language. It was developed as a part of IBM's DeepQA project by a research team, led by principal investigator David Ferrucci. Watson was named after IBM's founder and first CEO, industrialist Thomas J. Watson.
6 Jeopardy! is an American television game show created by Merv Griffin. The show is a quiz competition that reverses the traditional question-and-answer format of many quiz shows.
7 ChatGPT is a chatbot developed by OpenAI and launched on 30 November 2022. Based on large language models, it enables users to refine and steer a conversation towards a desired length, format, style, level of detail and language.
8 www.verygoodcopy.com/workforce-blog-3/the-hazards-of-busy-work.
9 And 'no', I in no way put myself anywhere near their stratospheric level.

Chapter 2

Behind the Laziness

We kick this off by making the point that all this laziness idea actually has both some science and some intelligence behind it, and is not just make-believe, we explore various historical characters such a Moltke and Pareto, as well as Baloo the Bear in *The Jungle Book*.

All of which will lead the reader to a decision point with three options open to them – leave, skip, continue. The choice is entirely yours. Go ahead, make your day.[1]

Note

1 "Go ahead, make my day" is a catchphrase from the 1983 film Sudden Impact, spoken by the character Harry Callahan, played by Clint Eastwood, one of the author's favourite actors and directors.

DOI: 10.4324/9781003506522-4

Productive lazy basics

Being lazy doesn't equate to being unintelligent. Instead, productive laziness entails achieving success with less effort. When I advocate for 'lazy' project management, I'm not suggesting we do nothing at all. Sitting around idly would be foolish and detrimental to our careers. Lazy, in this context, doesn't imply stupidity.

Rather, I propose a more focused approach to project management. It's about directing our efforts where they truly count, rather than busying ourselves with trivial tasks that others could handle or that don't require attention at all. Welcome to the concept of 'Productive Laziness'.

On the following pages, I delve deeper into what productive laziness means and how you can implement these strategies in your own projects. I'm not inherently lazy, but I recognize the importance of balancing work with other aspects of life. My goal is success, both in my projects and in maintaining a fulfilling personal life.

Lazy doesn't lead to failure. As a Lazy Project Manager, I've learned to strike this balance effectively, ensuring successful outcomes for my projects and my career alike, while still leaving time for family and personal pursuits. So, you can stick to the frantic pace of traditional project management, or you can join me in the pursuit of efficient success from the comfort of life's metaphorical comfy chair.

DOI: 10.4324/9781003506522-5

The science behind the laziness

This isn't just a whimsical notion; behind this theory lies a foundation of science, history and even a singing bear.

The Pareto Principle[1], commonly known as the 80/20 rule, suggests that for many occurrences, 80 per cent of the outcomes stem from 20 per cent of the causes. While this principle finds practical application in numerous scenarios, it's often misused. Merely fitting 80 per cent of cases doesn't automatically qualify a solution as adhering to the 80/20 rule; it's crucial to recognise that such a solution requires only 20 per cent of the resources needed to address all cases.

Originally proposed by management thinker Joseph M. Juran, the principle bears the name of Italian economist Vilfredo Pareto, who noted that 80 per cent of Italy's property was owned by 20 per cent of its population. The underlying assumption is that a small number of causes predominantly drive the results in any given situation.

For instance, "20 per cent of clients may account for 80 per cent of sales volume". While not absolute, this approximation is often fairly accurate and can inform future decision-making. The Pareto Principle extends beyond business into everyday life: we might find that we wear our favorite 20 per cent of clothes about 80 per cent of the time or spend 80 per cent of our time with just 20 per cent of our acquaintances. Many companies receive 80 per cent of their revenue from 20 per cent of customers.

It's important to distinguish the Pareto Principle from Pareto efficiency, which was indeed introduced by Pareto himself. His contributions to economics, sociology and moral philosophy, particularly in income distribution and individual choice analysis, are noteworthy. The principle reminds us, project managers, to focus on the vital 20 per cent.

Woody Allen[2] once quipped that "80 per cent of success is showing up", but I've witnessed projects where mere physical presence didn't equate to progress let alone any success. Instead, it's better to recognize that only 20 per cent of our daily tasks truly matter, yielding 80 per cent of our results.

DOI: 10.4324/9781003506522-6

Identifying and prioritising these tasks is the essence of 'Productive Laziness,' ensuring efficient outcomes with minimal effort.

Notes

1   The Pareto principle (also known as the 80/20 rule, the law of the vital few and the principle of factor sparsity states that for many outcomes, roughly 80 per cent of consequences come from 20 per cent of causes (the "vital few"). In 1941 management consultant Joseph M. Juran developed the concept in the context of quality control and improvement after reading the works of Italian sociologist and economist Vilfredo Pareto, who wrote in 1906 about the 80/20 connection while teaching at the University of Lausanne.[3] In his first work, *Cours d'économie politique*, Pareto showed that approximately 80 percent of the land in the Kingdom of Italy was owned by 20 per cent of the population. The Pareto principle is only tangentially related to Pareto efficiency.
2   Heywood Allen is an American filmmaker, actor and comedian whose career spans more than six decades. Allen has received many accolades, including the most nominations for the Academy Award for Best Original Screenplay.

The intelligence behind the laziness

It's not enough to simply embrace laziness; to truly excel, you must be lazy in a smart way. Productive Laziness isn't just about idleness; it's a powerful blend of laziness and intelligence. Those who master this combination possess a distinct advantage in society, especially in leadership roles within organizations.

This concept isn't new; it has historical roots, notably demonstrated in the Prussian army by Helmuth Karl Bernhard Graf von Moltke, a revered strategist of the 19th century. Moltke revolutionised military tactics during his tenure as chief of the Prussian army, implementing modern methods of army direction.

Moltke's approach to categorising his officer corps remains influential today, applicable not only to military leadership but also to project management and other forms of leadership. He divided officers into four distinct types, based on their mental and physical attributes.

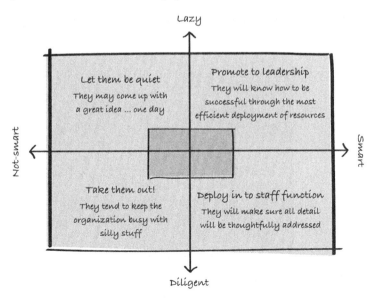

Figure 2.3.1 Moltke's categorization.

DOI: 10.4324/9781003506522-7

Type A officers, mentally dull and physically lazy, were assigned straightforward tasks but offered little potential for advancement. Type B officers, bright and energetic, tended to micromanage and lacked leadership qualities. Type C officers, dull but energetic, posed challenges requiring constant supervision and were often dismissed.

However, it was the Type D officers, mentally bright yet physically lazy, whom Moltke deemed most suitable for high command. These individuals possessed the intelligence to understand what needed to be done but were motivated by their laziness to seek the most efficient solutions. In essence, they epitomised success through minimal effort.

So, which type do you aspire to be? Type A, B, C or D? It's a challenging choice, indeed.

Smart lazy individuals hold a significant advantage and are ideally suited for leadership positions. *The Lazy Project Manager* embraces these principles, assuming the reader possesses intelligence and aims to refine their lazy skills to ascend to the top right-hand side of Moltke's diagram. By doing so, not only will projects become more successful, but individuals will also be recognised as competent leaders, primed for future roles.

In the words of Walter Chrysler[1], "Whenever there is a hard job to be done, I assign it to a lazy man; he is sure to find an easy way of doing it".

Note

1 Walter Percy Chrysler was an American industrial pioneer and executive in the automotive industry and the founder and namesake of American Chrysler Corporation.

The 'Goldilocks' equation

There is a word 'lagom' that you most probably have not heard of, unless you are Scandinavian – it's meaning kind of summarises this whole productive laziness thing.

'Lagom' is a Swedish term that means 'just the right amount' or 'not too much, not too little'. It can be translated in various ways, such as 'in moderation', 'in balance', 'perfect-simple', 'just enough' 'ideal', and 'suitable' (in terms of quantities). Unlike words like 'sufficient' and 'average', which imply some level of abstinence, scarcity or failure, 'lagom' conveys a sense of appropriateness, though not necessarily perfection. The quintessential Swedish proverb 'Lagom är bäst', literally 'The right amount is best' is also translated as 'Enough is as good as a feast', or 'There is virtue in moderation'.

It can be thought of as the 'Goldilocks[1]' equation, where what you have is not too much, not too little, but just right.

Think of Goldilocks when you are considering your own efforts and outputs.

Note

1 *Goldilocks and the Three Bears* is a 19th-century English fairy tale with three versions. The original tale features an impudent old woman who intrudes into the forest home of three anthropomorphic bachelor bears while they are away. She eats some of their porridge, sits on one of their chairs and breaks it and sleeps in one of their beds. When the bears return and find her, she wakes up, jumps out of the window and is never seen again. The second version replaces the old woman with a young, naive, blonde-haired girl named Goldilocks. The third and most famous version changes the bachelor bears to a family of three. This story has inspired various interpretations and has been adapted into films, operas and other media. *Goldilocks and the Three Bears* remains one of the most popular fairy tales in the English language.

DOI: 10.4324/9781003506522-8

A final definition

It's a kind of magic: when one plus one equals so much more than two.

What do you get when you cross one of the seven deadly sins with an accelerant for resource usage?

lazy [l'eɪzi]
adjective (lazier; laziest)

1. If someone is lazy, they do not want to work or make any effort to do anything.

   Lazy and incompetent workers are letting the company down.
   I was too lazy to learn how to read music.

   • **laziness** noun

Current employment laws will be changed to reward effort and punish laziness.

2. You can use **lazy** to describe an activity or event in which you are very relaxed and which you do or take part in without making much effort.

   Her latest novel is perfect for a lazy summer's afternoon reading.
   We would have a lazy lunch and then lie on the beach in the sun.

   • **lazily** adverb

Lisa went back into the kitchen, stretching lazily.

3. If you describe something as **lazy**, you mean that it moves or flows slowly and gently.

   A valley of rolling farms spread out along a lazy river.

   • **lazily** adverb

The river threaded its way lazily between the old city and the new.

DOI: 10.4324/9781003506522-9

Laziness, sloth: apathy and inactivity in the practice of virtue (personified as one of the deadly sins).

So lazy, or laziness, is mostly seen as a negative term, or at the very best, a term of selfish indulgence.

Productiveness, however, is seen as a very positive term: the ratio of work produced in a given period of time. Productivity relates to the person's ability to produce the standard amount or number of products, services or outcomes as described in a work description.

So, put the benefits of productiveness together with an intelligent application of laziness, and you get 'Productive Laziness'.

Or to put it another way, you get the maximum output for any given input, with an eye to minimizing the input as well. Or, to put it yet another way, you get a lot of bang for your bucks as some like to say!

It's a jungle (book) out there

Doo be doo be doo: Inspiration from a great 'character' actor.

You know that scene from The Jungle Book, one of Disney's great films[1], where the bear, Baloo, encourages Mowgli, the boy child, to think about life in a different way?

Baloo sings about looking for just the bare necessities of life, about trying to relax and cool it and not spending any time looking for things that are worth it or can't even be found. Or put it another way, he is explaining to Mowgli that life using the good old 80/20 rule can be a lot less stressful.

For me, 'The Bare Necessities' could well be the 'Productive Lazy' theme tune. Check out the full lyrics some time, take a stroll down memory lane and watch the film one more time and enjoy Baloo the (singing) Bear teach you all about the bare necessities of life that will come to you.

If that isn't good old doo be doo be doo productive laziness, I don't what is!

Note

1 *The Jungle Book* is a 1967 animated feature film, released on 18 October 1967. The 19th animated feature in the Disney animated features canon, it was the last to be produced by Walt Disney, who died during its production. It was inspired by the stories about the feral child Mowgli from the book of the same name by Rudyard Kipling. The movie remains one of Disney's most popular, and contained a number of classic songs, including 'The Bare Necessities' and 'I Wanna Be Like You'. Most of the songs were written by Richard M. Sherman and Robert B. Sherman.

DOI: 10.4324/9781003506522-10

Caveat emptor

Buyer Beware!

Let's make this crystal clear: what this book is, and what it absolutely is not.

Understanding the concept of 'Productive Laziness' is paramount, as is defining its scope and what it does not entail.

First, this is not your typical project management training manual. It won't teach you the ins and outs of project management; if you're looking to delve into critical path analysis, earned value management or work breakdown structures, this book isn't the one for you. Instead, you might want to reach for that allegedly more mundane-looking tome nearby.

Similarly, it doesn't serve as a replacement for a comprehensive project management education programme. There are undoubtedly significant aspects of the project management skill set and process that are not covered here.

Nor is it an alternative to a structured project management methodology. Absolutely not.

And it certainly doesn't substitute for experience or the guidance of an experienced project management coach. These are things you should already have in place or be actively pursuing.

However, what this book does offer is a sharing of personal experiences. It can act as a virtual coach, to some extent, guiding you through your project work.

It outlines a smarter way of working.

When applied effectively, it can enhance productivity both within your projects and beyond. It can help you achieve a better work–life balance.

This approach has proven successful for me and may do the same for you. Just to reiterate, I've undergone formal training in various project management methodologies, I'm a certified PMP® through PMI, and I've accumulated extensive practical experience over three decades across diverse projects and industries, with the support of excellent project managers along the way.

DOI: 10.4324/9781003506522-11

So, what is being a Lazy Project Manager all about?

It's about honing your focus in project management efforts and directing your energy where it truly counts, where it can make the most significant impact.

There are countless books that delve into the minutiae of project management; this isn't one of them[1]. Consider this project management from a high-altitude perspective.

Welcome to the project management 'mile-high' club!

Note

1 When I first wrote *The Lazy Project Manager* I was, I have to admit, inspired to write something that wasn't just plain boring – as most of the project management books were then (it has improved somewhat but not as much as you might hope – I am not one for the heavy tome, the wise and worthy thoughts of the elitist author years removed from actually doing the bloody job). There, I feel better now.

Decision point – Can I cheat?

So you are already thinking in the 'productive lazy' way?

That combination of inherent intelligence and underlying laziness is kicking in already.

Well, good for you!

You are wondering if you really have to read the whole book through, study the contents carefully, connect with each idea and experiment in your daily project life in order to reach the higher plane of conscientiousness that is 'Productive Laziness'.

You are thinking that that seems like an awful lot of hard work considering this book is supposedly teaching you take it easy in the comfy chair.

Or maybe you are one of those people who just have to skip to the end and see what happens. Or maybe you want to just validate the value of the book before investing any more of your overly hard worked for money by seeing some sort of summary and conclusion.

Possibly you are a student of project management who, having left some piece of work right to the very last moment again, is rushing to grab as many salient points and quotes on this subject as possible, with as little actual effort as possible, in order to both meet a deadline and to achieve an acceptable grade.

Whatever the reasons, and in the extremely selfish interests of a potential book sale, here is the answer you are looking for.

Yes!

Yes, you can cheat.

Yes, you can skip all the way to chapter which is entitled 'Quick Tips to Productive Lazy Heaven' and/or 'Quick Tips to Productive Personal Heaven'.

And yes, there you will find what you are looking for. Much time saved but perhaps an experience missed.

Also, just before you head off to the end of the book, I do hope that you will return to the next chapter at some point, partly because it does set the scene for the structure of the book (and the Quick Tips), partly because there are many wise words and ideas covered that will help you in the future,

DOI: 10.4324/9781003506522-12

and also partly because I have spent a long time writing this and will probably sulk if you don't.

OK, decision time. See you on the next page or later on near the end of the book.

Chapter 3

The Dinosaur Theory

Where we finally get to the part that explains why a project management book has a dinosaur on the cover, you have probably been wondering about this but hey, it got you to at least pick up the book didn't it. And we delve into what the actual dinosaur theory is all about.

The author also has a second theory, but that is hardly surprising if you knew him at all.

DOI: 10.4324/9781003506522-13

An alternative view to the traditional one

Richard Owen[1] may have got it wrong.

This book is structured around a particular theory that I have. It is my theory and no one else's and it goes like this.

Are you ready?

Good.

Here we go then.

Theory by Miss Anne Elk:

'All brontosauruses are thin at one end, much, much thicker in the middle, and then thin again at the far end. That is the theory that I have and which is mine, and what it is too'. Monty Python[2,3]

Figure 3.1.1 A dinosaur.

The Lazy Project Manager's Theory of Projects, from a Productive Laziness aspect:

"All projects are thick at one end, much, much thinner in the middle and then thick again at the far end. That is the theory that I have and which is mine, and what it is too".

DOI: 10.4324/9781003506522-14

Figure 3.1.2 A project dinosaur.

The point here is that, working by the productive lazy rule, a smart project manager should apply time and effort at the critical stages of a project, i.e. the start and the finish, and less time in the middle or the less critical stage. At this stage there are others in the project who should be doing most of the hard work, and you probably deserve a bit of a rest anyway.

I do have a second theory (as did Miss Anne Elk by the way):

'If you want to get a brontosaurus from 'a' to 'b' then you ride the dinosaur – you don't carry it!'

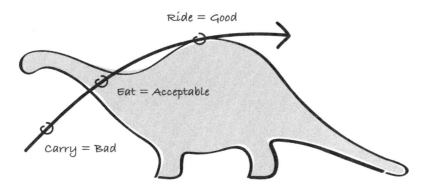

Figure 3.1.3 A good project dinosaur.

And the point this time is that as a smart project manager you should be directing the project and not trying to pick it up and carry its heavy, heavy load on your back all the way to the delivery gate. That way only failure, backache and heartache lie.

The following chapters of this book lay out suggestions for ways to apply the 80/20 rule in your projects and to your personal life so that you can 'work smarter' and enjoy the rewards of 'Productive Laziness'.

It should also be remembered that it is as much to do about what you don't 'do' as to what you do 'do'. Do the things that will contribute to the '80 per cent' and avoid doing the things that won't.

We will start at the beginning, of course, where the Lazy Project Manager's Theory of Projects, from a Productive Laziness aspect, states that 'All projects are thick at one end …', but first let's consider the all too important aspect of personal productivity since the two go hand in.

Notes

1 Sir Richard Owen KCB FRMS FRS was an English biologist, comparative anatomist and palaeontologist. Owen is generally considered to have been an outstanding naturalist with a remarkable gift for interpreting fossils.
2 Monty Python were a British comedy troupe formed in 1969 consisting of Graham Chapman, John Cleese, Terry Gilliam, Eric Idle, Terry Jones and Michael Palin. The group came to prominence for the sketch comedy series Monty Python's Flying Circus, which aired on the BBC from 1969 until 1974.
3 Check out the video of this sketch here: https://youtu.be/cAYDiPizDIs?si= FOBUmBQGAtx0U7p_.

Chapter 4

Productivity Practice

Here we delve into the unique challenge of being a truly successful and productive lazy project manager, emphasising the importance of managing oneself while overseeing projects. It discusses the evolution of the concept of productive laziness, intertwining personal productivity insights with project management principles.

Through a somewhat unusual (for project management books) narrative featuring a prehistoric protagonist named Ug, we explore the instinctive responses to stress and the implications for effective communication. Stress, both physiological and psychological, is examined, alongside the detrimental effects of the amygdala's dominance in 'fight or flight' situations. Underscoring the necessity of foresight and urging project managers to embrace preparedness and avoid surprises. Ultimately, by adopting a proactive approach to planning and communication, individuals can achieve success with minimal effort, embodying the essence of productive laziness.

DOI: 10.4324/9781003506522-15

A unique challenge

Being a truly successful productively lazy project manager is a unique challenge in many ways.

The best description I ever had of the original *Lazy Project Manager* book was that is a book that showed you how to manage yourself whilst managing projects[1].

To that end, when I started speaking on project management and productive laziness it became clear that people wanted more guidance and more help in changing their own ways of working – what is now regularly thought of as achieving and great work/life balance.

Therefore this book interweaves personal productivity ideas throughout, based on all my work in the area of being a lazy winner, reducing effort and succeeding in people's work and personal life without rushing around like a headless chicken or putting in 100-hour weeks.

It takes readers on a path that explores the 'journey' of personal change, the 'change' itself (and all the inevitable challenges with that) and concludes with a vision of what the 'destination' could be.

We are all too good to put our personal life and careers and work–life balance at risk by working too hard! Equally we can't head off in the opposite direction and ignore the 'work' part of the equation while focusing our time and effort solely on the 'life' part. That is not a work–life balance at all and just won't work for the majority of people, unless you are already wealthy enough to go for just a life–life balance[2].

Notes

1 David mentioned this in the foreword.
2 Then you do need to come up with a real 'balance' that applies to you.

DOI: 10.4324/9781003506522-16

Dealing with the 'F' word

No I am not getting all 'Anglo-Saxon' and aggressive but rather reflective on a presentation I delivered – titled 'The F-Word[1]'.

This is all about the issue of lack of foresight, the 'F' word in this instance is both quite innocuous but also very important, for a lazy but productive person.

The conference theme I presented under was in fact 'Fight, Flight or Freeze' and this is what inspired me to consider these responses and validate that they were aligned to the spirit of 'The Lazy Project Manager'.

There are actually four responses to a stress situation, or imminent danger event:

- Freeze
- Flight
- Fight
- Fawn

The fourth was named by Pete Walker[2], a therapist who said 'I have named it the fawn response…the fourth 'f' in the fight/flight/ freeze/fawn repertoire of instinctive responses to trauma. Fawn, according to Webster's, means: to act servilely; cringe and flatter'.

To explain this further to my audience I used a mammoth vs caveman situation back in pre-history, the dawn of the would-be Lazy Project Manager/ Caveman/Hunter.

Ug, let us call our caveman Ug for the sake of a name, was pretty fed up. He went out each day to hunt for food for his family and tribe members, and each day, after many hours, he would return home with a small mammal of some sort, and each day his family and tribe members would consume the food and demand more for tomorrow. And so the next day Ug would have to do it all over again. No rest. No time to himself. And yet, budding deep inside Ug was the makings of a 'Lazy' (in a good way) man.

DOI: 10.4324/9781003506522-17

One day, as he gazed down across the plains from the cliff side where he and his family and tribe lived in the caves, he stared at the herd of mammoth wandering around and eating.

It suddenly came to him – if he could kill a mammoth his family, tribe and pretty much anyone else who might wander past the caves at mealtimes would eat for days and days and he, Ug, could take a well-earned rest.

And so Ug hatched a plan to kill a mammoth.

To be honest, it wasn't a good plan, but it was his plan and the next day saw Ug action his less than well-thought through plan by striding down the hillside with a large stone club in one hand and a large spear in the other.

He headed directly for the first mammoth and with a loud war cry that attracted the attention of all of Ug's family and friends, not to mention the attention of all of the mammoths nearby, Ug hurled his club at the head of the mammoth. The club flew through the air and bounced off the mammoth's large hairy skull.

This resulted in two things. First, Ug now only had one weapon left, the spear, and second, Ug had the full and undivided attention of the rather large mammoth with the three-metre-long tusks, eight tonnes of body weight and a minor headache.

Ug moved on to stage two of his unfortunately unimpressive plan and threw the spear at the same mammoth, again with a mighty war cry. Up on the hillside his family members cheered (hopefully) at Ug's bravery.

This resulted in only one thing that really mattered.

Ug was facing a charging mammoth of significant size coming at him at impressive speed and he now had only four options:

- Freeze: not so good in this case, as the mammoth is in front of Ug and heading his way (at speed and with a real purpose)
- Fawn: you rarely want to pet a mammoth in any situation, and this was definitely a 'situation' where petting was inappropriate
- Fight: well, Ug better have quite a few friends with a lot more weapons willing to join in the fight really fast, and in reality, these were all still up on the hillside loudly discussing the situation Ug had managed to get himself in to
- Flight: sounds the most sensible in this situation, live to 'FFFF' another day!

History will allow us to fast-forward some months and see Ug, the now truly 'Lazy Project Manager', with a significantly improved plan born out of vivid personal experience overseeing an organised activity with all of the male tribe members driving a mammoth isolated from the herd towards a pre-selected cliff edge to fall to certain death ready for the hunters to recover the body. Fast-forward a few hours from that, and we can see Ug and all of his family members feasting on roasted mammoth and Ug looking forward to a few weeks rest and relaxation before his next hunting trip – hunting smarter and not harder!

Flight in this case was the right choice, but there is another F-Word that Ug should have considered before that almost fateful first attempt at mammoth hunting.

Now consider yourself, you have a body – lots of it, inside and out, and when faced with a high-risk situation, what happens to your body?

(Warning – this is the science bit)

A reaction begins in the amygdala, which triggers a neural response in the hypothalamus. The initial reaction is followed by activation of the pituitary gland and secretion of the hormone ACTH. The adrenal gland is activated almost simultaneously and releases the neurotransmitter epinephrine. The release of chemical messengers results in the production of the hormone cortisol, which increases blood pressure and blood sugar and suppresses the immune system. The initial response and subsequent reactions are triggered in an effort to create a boost of energy. This boost of energy is activated by epinephrine binding to liver cells and the subsequent production of glucose.

Additionally, the circulation of cortisol functions to turn fatty acids into available energy, which:

- Acceleration of heart and lung action
- Paling or flushing, or alternating between both
- Inhibition of stomach and upper-intestinal action to the point where digestion slows down or stops
- General effect on the sphincters of the body
- Constriction of blood vessels in many parts of the body
- Liberation of metabolic energy sources for muscular action
- Dilation of blood vessels for muscles
- Inhibition of the lacrimal gland (responsible for tear production and salivation)
- Dilation of pupil
- Relaxation of bladder
- Inhibition of erection
- Auditory exclusion (loss of hearing)
- Tunnel vision (loss of peripheral vision)
- Disinhibition of spinal reflexes
- Shaking

Do you recognise any of this? I certainly do.

Notes

1 Well you can't accuse me of not going for the attention-grabbing headlines in my book.
2 Pete Walker coined the term fawn and defined it through the following: "The Fawn response is one of four defensive reactions to ongoing trauma. Those who fawn tend to put the needs and wants of others ahead of themselves at the cost of the health of their own egos, and the protection of and compassion for themselves." From: http://www.pete-walker.com/fourFs_TraumaTypologyComplex PTSD.htm.

Stress and mental health

I ran a significant project in the early days of my project management career, and, to put it simply, I made myself pretty ill as a result. I was so focused and so involved in, well, 'everything', that I suffered from stress both during and after the project ended. I did neither myself nor the project any good acting this way.

There are many negative effects of stress:

- Physiological effects
- Headaches
- Muscle tension and pain
- Chest pain
- Fatigue
- Changes in sex drive
- Upset stomach
- Problems with sleeping
- Urinary problems
- Psychological effects
- Anxiety
- Restlessness
- Lack of motivation or focus
- Irritability or anger
- Depression
- Behavioural effects
- Over-eating or under-eating
- Drug or alcohol abuse
- Social withdrawal

Stress is, in the short term, a good thing in that those instinctive responses to trauma kick in, and we move into survival mode rapidly and go for our selected 'F' response, but stress in anything but the short term is a bad thing, as I found out to my own personal cost.

DOI: 10.4324/9781003506522-18

But I learnt from the experience, and this led me to the revised behaviour that forms the basis of *The Lazy Project Manager* – just like Ug, I learnt from the bad experience and changed the way I acted.

And there is more – It has to do with the 'fight or flight' gland in our brain, the amygdala mentioned earlier. As it turns out, this little gland has significant implications for project communications.

When the amygdala 'takes over' in a 'fight or flight' situation, we almost instantly lose the ability to do three things:

- Empathise
- Reason
- Listen

Given how crucial those three things are to productive and constructive communications (both personal and professional!), we need to be pragmatic and realistic about our communications, whenever we are angry or very stressed. Specifically, we might need to give ourselves a 'time out' by not sending that email, or making that phone call or continuing a heated 'discussion' with our significant other or our work colleague.

One last piece of advice – there is a real risk with regards to the 'Fight' syndrome option. Used successfully in one situation, there is a real possibility of a future addiction to this option in the next situation and the one after that and so on. You face a tough situation and select fight mode, and as a result you win the day or get want you want – you feel great! And so you respond the same next time around, and there is no longer a possibility for any other response, and this doesn't make for a good project manager (or person).

And so on the real 'F-Word', the one I want to talk about, the one that our caveman friend Ug should have used, the fifth 'F'.

This F-Word is 'Foresight' – the greatest strength a project manager has is to be prepared.

I was given some great advice when I started out from my manager and that was 'No surprises' – he said that he would support me in all situations, as long as he was pre-warned by me. He didn't expect me to be perfect and he knew there would be problems at times, but as long as I was the one telling him about the issue or challenge first, he was confident that I was in control but if someone else told him first then I perhaps wasn't.

So 'No surprises' is a good motto for all project managers.

And that is where 'Productive Laziness' comes in – working smarter and not harder – being well prepared and therefore being capable of dealing with anything.

Go forward use the F-Word wisely and have foresight!

With a different approach to planning, you can ensure that you are one of the lazy winners in life and achieve success in what you do at work and beyond – achieving more impressive results with the minimum of effort.

Chapter 5

Laziness – Thick at One End

In the thick of project initiation lies a pivotal moment for any project manager labelled as 'lazy'.

Amid the challenges of launching a project, it's crucial to discern where to focus energy and attention. This chapter delves into the nuances of this initial phase, exploring the key areas that demand the discerning eye of a supposedly productively lazy project manager.

We also navigate through the back end of initiation, where we uncover the strategic manoeuvres and subtle moves that can lay the groundwork for project success. So, fasten your seatbelt as we embark on a journey through the thick front end of project management, where lethargy meets strategy, and laziness finds purpose.

DOI: 10.4324/9781003506522-19

Thick at one end

Where do you begin and with what, and after that what next?

So what is it that a 'lazy' project manager should focus on during this initial 'thick' front end to their projects? And by front end, if you happen to be following this is real project management terminology, then I am referring to initiation of the project. Well, the back end of initiation anyway. There is a project, you are the project manager, and the project is kicking off. Like I said, the 'thick' front-end.

So what is it that should get you out of the 'comfy chair' and rushing in to action?

Well, first getting ahead, and then staying ahead, of the 'game'. Then planning a strategy for managing the two critical 'players' in any project – the project sponsor, who should be known at this point, and the project creep, who will be unknown but could be anyone or everyone, including, if you are really unlucky, the project sponsor, or, if you are really stupid, you.

And finally, the project manager needs to be planning for zero communication breakdowns, a singularly significant activity, since general guidance suggests that some 70 per cent of your time as a project manager should be spent in some form of communication or other.

Three areas to focus on to ensure the project, that is your project, starts off in the right way, in the right direction, and at the right momentum, and with the right processes and controls in place.

There is a well-known project maxim that says 'Projects don't fail at the end. They fail at the beginning'.

Failure at the beginning is just harder to spot and hurts a lot less, for a while at least.

'A bad beginning makes a bad ending'.

Euripides[1]

DOI: 10.4324/9781003506522-20

Note

1 Euripides was a tragedian of classical Athens. Along with Aeschylus and Sophocles, he is one of the three ancient Greek tragedians for whom any plays have survived in full. Some ancient scholars attributed 95 plays to him, but the Suda says it was 92 at most.

Ahead of the Game

Start the way you mean to carry on and carry on the way you mean to finish.

Typically, when a project manager arrives at the start of a brand shiny new project, they will enter a point in time that is full of peace and love and general wellbeing between all parties involved. The sales cycle will be out of the way, if external suppliers are involved, the celebration parties will still be fond memories with people enthusiastically sharing embarrassing photographs on intranet sites, and everyone will believe that this is going to be a fantastic success with riches for all involved just around the corner. This project will be different from all the other projects.

Chaos reports[1] will be relegated to waste bins, and the world will be a smiley happy one where optimism abounds.

But we all know the reality of project history and the typical phases that projects experience:

1. Enthusiasm
2. Total Confusion
3. Disillusionment
4. Search for the Guilty
5. Punishment of the Innocent
6. Reward and Promotion of the Non-participants

Obviously, you want to avoid this scenario; you want to be a success. Therefore this is not a time for the project manager to indulge in laziness; this will come later. No, for now, this is a time when the project manager will be busy and visible and will stamp their authority on the project right from the very first moment, the very first phone call, the very first meeting, and the very first time they step in to the project office.

It is at this point that the project can be won or lost for a project manager because it is now, and only now, that they will have to opportunity to drive and structure the project the way they want to.

DOI: 10.4324/9781003506522-21

It is important to let everyone know that you have arrived and that you demand that things are done your way, the right way, the way that is best for the project. Equally it is important that you educate your project team on why this is required and what the benefits are that can be achieved by working your way – for them, for you and for the project.

Productive laziness will follow, but for now take control and work hard. Now you need to understand exactly what you have taken on, or landed with, if this project was not actively selected by you. Now you need information, and you will have many questions to ask and many answers to uncover.

And one word of warning before we start, there is a project management 'law' that says 'Attempts to get answers early in a project fail as there are many more wrong questions than right ones. Activity during the early stages should be dedicated to finding the correct questions. Once the correct questions have been identified, correct answers will naturally fall out of subsequent work without grief or excitement, and there will be understanding of what the project is meant to achieve'. This is known as Hoggarth's Law.

Wise words indeed, I think Hoggarth had the makings of a lazy project manager. Do not waste time – be productive, but in 'lazy' way.

Note

1 The Standish Group regularly produces the CHAOS reports, which research the reasons for IT project failure in the United States. Personally I'm not a great fan, and, from my own experience, the rate of success in project management is far higher that CHAOS (and others) regularly report.

Applying the 'Productive Lazy' approach

Start as you mean to go on

It means you should begin any new enterprise by acting and sounding as if it were already a success and by setting the standards you both expect and need to make that enterprise a success. In this case, your project is the enterprise, and you have every intention of making a success of it. Non-negotiable; this is what it will be, and failure is not an option. Your very attitude as you assume control for this change process will inform others that they are joining a winning team setting out on a journey than will end in a sunset of success.

Confidence does breed success

Show you mean business by ensuring that all parties involved in the project both understand what you need and expect from them and also in what format you expect it, whether this is information, time, support, guidance or money. Not in an aggressive way but in an authoritative way.

As part of this process it is equally important to explain to people why it is in their interest to deliver what you ask and to deliver it in the manner in which you request. Time now for some education, if needed, on what is good for the project is good for the project team members.

Dress for success

Dress the part as well. Even if you have members in your team who you have worked with before making it clear at the start of any new project who is the project manager. Dressing to show this can help present your status and therefore authority. Now I am not suggesting building yourself a small throne in the project office and putting on a nice ermine cloak with a crown or anything crazy like that. No, just dress smartly and behave correctly. It is surprising, even in a casual working environment, putting on a suit and tie[1]

DOI: 10.4324/9781003506522-22

or smart suit and blouse can adjust your attitude in a positive way. Maybe try it once a month if it is not the norm, or for steering meetings, whatever you feel is appropriate.

Note: Yes, of course the world has moved on, and projects can be partly or wholly remote-/virtual-led, but this leads to a greater danger, I feel, in that we all get so relaxed about dress code and image. I'm really not proposing wearing a suit on a Zoom or Teams call, but just think about the image you are projecting. I vary mine according to the meeting type.

Paint the picture of the journey

It is also critical that you, as the project expert, clearly explain the journey that you and the project team and stakeholders will travel for the next few weeks or months.

Lay out when, what, why and how everything will roll out in the coming period of time right up to project (successful) end.

Got a methodology or framework? Then share it openly.

Get the upper hand

Getting the upper hand is always a great start to any project (in a nice way, or in a less than nice way, if you have to).

Not everybody will accept your authority at the very start of a project. A good way to gain the upper hand in this is to ensure that others, who you may have identified already as those that you might have some problems with, have deliverables very early on in the project. Now, if they should perhaps happen to be challenging deliverables that say maybe they don't deliver on, then you might say 'all the better'. If they fail, then they are the naughty ones from the very start of the project.

Don't let them escape from their commitments or expected deliverables. I'm not saying set them up, not in so many words anyway, but take the opportunities as you see fit and use your experience to your advantage. Add to that maybe a few deliverables that are easy for you, and your team, to deliver and then you have the upper hand for sure. Quick wins can be good things, for you.

Another way to make sure that your authority is not challenged is to be prepared – like the scouts of your childhood – be ready. Have that all-purpose penknife handy, you know, the one with the thingy that gets stones out of horse's hoofs. Well at least have the project management equivalent of a Swiss Army knife ready, cleaned and polished to hand, just in case you need it.

Be prepared

Be prepared and know your facts. Ensure you know all the facts you can in advance – do some research and have it on hand ready to produce. Most people usually fail to prepare their facts; they dominate meetings and conversations through sheer force and reputation. If you know and can produce facts to support or defend your position, it is unlikely that anyone will have anything prepared in response. When you know that a situation is going to arise, over which you'd like to have some influence, prepare your facts, do your research, do the sums, get the facts and figures, gather opinions and views, and be able to quote sources; then you will be able to make a firm case and also dramatically improve your reputation for being someone who is organised and firm, someone who is in control and who should be listened to and respected.

Anticipate everything you can

Also try anticipating other people's behaviour and prepare your own responses accordingly. This is not so easy at the start of a project as often you will not know the characteristics of the people involved. But you can prepare your responses according to the likely different scenarios that you think could be presented to you. Make sure your close project team are with you on this as well. You are not alone in all of this. Involve the resources you have to hand and listen to what they have to say. Use them to help secure the position of strength and dominance that you want at this critical stage.

Don't just anticipate the people side of the project, anticipate what you can about the technical side, the business side, any external influences, anything, and everything you can. Spending some time just thinking through the project timeline and considering possible issues or risks that may occur is a very productive thing to do. By imagining what might happen and then considering what could happen to avert or reduce that issue or risk will put you in a good position for if, or when that does happen. Just like a chess player thinking many moves ahead.

Being well prepared will increase your perceived confidence and enable you to be assertive about what's important to you.

Know the 'end game'

Throughout this busy start-up of the project, it is critical that you both know and understand the 'end game' or the final expected deliverables that your project is desired to achieve. Admittedly, many projects are still evolving these throughout the project initiation phase and, with the advent of more agile project methods, these days these deliverables evolve (to a certain extent) throughout the project lifecycle.

But the 'end game' must be watched like a light at the end of the tunnel or a beacon on the shoreline. Distraction from the end point of the project will impact your ability to make critically correct decisions along the way, crucial ones at the very start of the project and your ability to direct the project in a steady and true path.

I guess this all sounds like a lot of work and counter-intuitive for the whole 'Productive Lazy' theme. Well believe me, this is an investment that is both critical and one that will pay huge dividends as the project progresses. It will allow you to become that lazy project manager and sit back in that comfy chair. But get on the back foot now, and the project will be running you from day two onwards; you will be carrying that dinosaur all the way to the end date. Conversely get it right now, and life will be so much easier for the rest of the project.

Note

1 OK, I'll come clean – apart from my own wedding, I haven't worn a tie in the past five years.

A project manager's tale where first impressions counted (against me)

As a young and inexperienced project manager I began working on a new project at a large Scottish based company. My job was to do all those things that I had been taught on my recent project management course. A good course but, like most courses, a course based on theory and documented best practice.

So I knew about kick off meetings, sponsors and steering meetings, scope control, issue management, risk management and mitigation, work break down structures, budgetary planning and all those really important things.

What I didn't know was that there was so much more to being a project manager.

What I did know was I had a smart new suit and tie and an extremely practical and shiny new business case for all my future project files. I was ready.

I left my offices and headed to the customer site. Now, in those days I worked for a small software house and, as part of the sale to this customer, my company could recognise some revenue upon delivery and installation of the software. Already on site was a technician who was installing the software but who needed some sort of software patch to solve a problem that they had come across.

So I left my offices, headed to the customer site, parked my car and, on the way to my first steering committee meeting, popped in to the IT department with the required tape[1] in my hands (my shiny new briefcase in the other hand, of course). Passing a group of people on the way over, I quickly made my delivery and headed back to the main building and in to the meeting room in plenty of time for my first steering meeting.

I was greeted by the chairman of the steering committee – a man I had passed only minutes before in the group outside as I made my way to the IT department.

'Who are you then?' he questioned, and when I explained that I was the project manager, he laughed 'I thought you were just some 'techie' who had got lost'.

DOI: 10.4324/9781003506522-23

Ouch! That hurt. All that training and preparation, not to mention the investment in the nice suit and briefcase, was gone completely to waste in a matter of seconds.

You know, even though he seemed say that all in good humour, it took me at least another six months to win his confidence that I was both a real project manager and that I knew what I was doing and could be trusted.

That first chance encounter had significant implications for me, and all because that first impression was not what I had planned, all because I was carrying a computer tape and therefore looked like a techie.

First impressions really count.

Make yours count the right way.

Note

1 For you youngsters out there, a magnetic tape for data storage was wound on large (10.5 in/26.67 cm) reels. This de facto standard for large computer systems persisted until the late 1980s.

Manage the Sponsor

How to control your greatest asset (and potentially your biggest threat)

Critical to any project's success is having a good project sponsor, but, like the saying goes 'you can pick your friends, but you can't pick your relatives', and the same is true of project sponsors.

So what makes a good project sponsor and how do you deal with the one you have just inherited for your project?

The Project Sponsor is the key stakeholder representative for the project and provides the necessary support for the Project Manager with the primary responsibility of achievement of the project objectives and benefits. An inappropriate choice of Project Sponsor can seriously impact the possibility of success of the project and provide you, the project manager, with an unwanted additional overhead.

Now you can't practically ask a sponsor for their CV[1] and put them through a formal interview process, nice as it would be sometimes to utter the phrase 'I'm sorry but I just don't think that this is the job for you right now'. But you should evaluate the sponsor you have and complete, in a subtle way of course, a 'Strengths and Weaknesses' assessment, so that you can adapt your project approach and communication methods to maximise their sponsorship support for the project that you now manage.

You can also openly discuss your intended plans for project management and communication to ensure that they fully buy-in to what you intend and how you intend to achieve it:. Responsibilities for project sponsors typically include:

- Providing direction and guidance for strategies and initiatives
- Negotiate funding for the project
- Actively participating in the initial project planning
- Identifying project Steering Committee members
- Working with the Project Manager to develop the Project Charter
- Identifying and quantifying business benefits to be achieved by successful implementation of the project

DOI: 10.4324/9781003506522-24

- Reviewing and approving changes to plans, priorities, deliverables, schedule, etc.
- Gaining agreement amongst the stakeholders when differences of opinion occur
- Assisting the project when required (especially in an 'out-of-control' situation) by exerting their organizational authority and ability to influence
- Assisting with the resolution of inter-project boundary issues
- Chairing the Project Steering Committee
- Supporting the Project Manager in conflict resolution
- Make the project visible in the organisation
- Encouraging stakeholder involvement and building and maintaining their ongoing commitment through effective communication strategies
- Advising the Project Manager of protocols, political issues, potential sensitivities, etc.
- Evaluating the project's success on completion

The shocking state of sponsorship today

In my book *Strategies for Project Sponsorship*[2], I, with my fellow authors, discovered some shocking statistics.

We found that the state of sponsorship could be summarised in just three numbers – 85; 83; and 100.

We surveyed a large number of organisations around the world, and they declared that 85 per cent had some form of recognised project sponsorship in place, and for this we used a very broad definition. You may wonder what the 15 per cent who were doing project-based work filled the gap but, hey, 85 per cent is a pretty good starting number.

But 83 per cent of those same companies admitted that they did absolutely nothing to support, train, guide, develop or help in any way the sponsors that they had in place. They just assumed to be able to do the 'job' because they were senior successful people!

And here is the 'killer', 100 per cent (well it was actually 99.5 per cent, but I am rounding up for simplicity) of those who responded said 'good project sponsorship' was critical to successful project outcomes.

Let me allow that to sink in for a while.

Notes

1 A résumé, also spelled resumé or resume (also called curriculum vitae or CV) is a document that contains a summary or listing of relevant job experience and education. The résumé or CV is typically the first item that a potential employer encounters regarding the job seeker and is typically used to screen applicants, often followed by an interview, when seeking employment.

2 www.amazon.co.uk/Strategies-Project-Sponsorship-Vicki-James/dp/1567264069.

Applying the 'Productive Lazy' approach

The Project Sponsor should be a senior manager having the financial and organisational power to act quickly and decisively in the overall governance of the project. It is an active, hands-on role, requiring a supportive working relationship with the Project Manager and effective communication with major stakeholders. The Project Sponsor should have a broad knowledge of the business including experience and expertise in the functional areas addressed by the project.

Applying the 'Productive Lazy' approach

Ask them what they expect

It is important to get the project off to a good start and build a strong relationship with the project sponsor. Don't take any second-hand statements, references, quotes or rumours to be the truth of the project sponsors views and expectations. Ask them. Clarify directly and take only their word for what it is they want and expect.

Now it may well be possible that the sponsor may not yet know what they expect. It may that this is their first time as a project sponsor and the role is as new to them as the project sponsor is to you. If that is the case, you need to help them and guide them in the responsibilities that they may have.

Either way, consider your first meeting with the sponsor, new or not so new to the role, known or unknown to you from previous projects. What would be reasonable to cover in such a meeting?

I joked that you couldn't practically ask a sponsor for their credentials for this job and put them through a formal interview process. Indeed, more often than not, the project sponsor has been chosen by the business well before you have even been selected as the project manager. But let's just assume that you can interview them, this could be fun.

'Tell me why you think you are the right person for this job?' – Well, what skills are you looking for in a good project sponsor?

DOI: 10.4324/9781003506522-25

'What strengths will you bring to the role?' – What are the strengths that would make your life as a project manager that much easier?

'What are your points of weakness and what action will you take to address these issues?' – What weaknesses are you looking to avoid at all costs?

Manage the first meeting

In preparing for that first meeting (interview) with your sponsor you will need to understand that some sponsors will have a very fixed vision for the project and will tell you, and the rest of the project team, exactly what they want, when they want it, and what will happen if they don't get what they want. Be cautious with these sponsors, their strength of purpose and character may challenge your interviewing skills. But it is still essential that you end up with the clarity of purpose that you need to run this project and work closely with the project sponsor.

Other project sponsors may have a vision that appears to be an undefined conceptual possibility developed with a small dose of delusion and aided (allegedly) with hint of illegal substance abuse.

OK then, so your sponsor will be somewhere between the above extremes (if you are lucky).

Ask the questions you need to ask

Well consider the following key topics; business objective(s), anticipated impact of the project deliverables, expected quality standards, significant risks seen at this stage, key dates on the project horizon, key stakeholders (beyond yourself and the project sponsor), and any budgetary constraints that are likely. In addition, you need to learn what style of communication and relationship this particular sponsor expects from you.

Just like in the previous chapter, first impressions really count so do your preparation well. If you conduct a good, professional, confident, first meeting with your project sponsor you will not only demonstrate your capability in a good light, but you will also provide a valuable service to the sponsor.

Open discussion works

'Tell me about the project we have'. Feel free to start the conversation in a simple way, with an open question, and then follow up with other questions that you need to ask in order to reach a suitable level of confidence in your understanding of those key topics; business objective(s), anticipated impact of the project deliverables, quality standards, significant risks seen at this stage, key dates on the project horizon, key stakeholders and budgetary constraints.

One tip here, you are only on an information gathering exercise right now. I know I said take the project with a firm hand from day one, but as far as the project sponsor is concerned, I would advise being a little gentle to begin with, at least until you understand what type of sponsor you are dealing with. You can put your firm grip in place and negotiate hard later on. Right now just learn and inwardly digest what you are told.

OK, now you need to go ahead and 'interview' the project sponsor. But what happens if they fail the interview? Consider first if remedial work can be put in place to help them 'raise their game', or alternatively, can you fill any deficiencies that you identify – either by process or resources? It the failure is so significant this will be a real project risk. I guess now only two options remain – this project ain't big enough for the both you, and one of you is gonna to have to leave town.

Once the interview is out of the way, maybe you can check their references, or maybe the next step is to get them to complete a psychometric test.

Here's one simple test you could try, just to help you filter out the extreme cases (answer at the end of this chapter). The question may or may not help with profiling your project sponsor but at the very least it is great fun at a project team social gathering.

A young woman[1] goes to the funeral of her mother. There she meets a man whom she has never met before. She identifies him as the man of her dreams and immediately falls in love with him. She has no idea who he is and no-one at the funeral has ever met him before or who knows who he is. Two weeks later she kills her sister. Why?

Apply the power grid

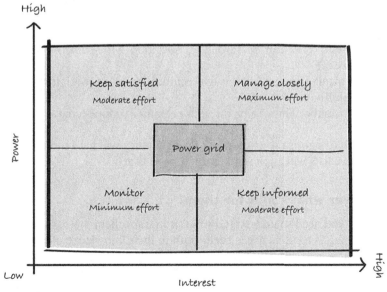

Figure 5.6.1 Power grid.

But let's not be pessimistic, that isn't going to happen to you, you won't get an extreme case of project sponsor, and they won't fail the 'interview'. So, what is your next move? Well perhaps you should consider the power base that your project sponsor has. Use the power grid below to assess your project sponsor, assess their rating of interest in this project from high to low and their actual power in the organisation, also from high to low.

This will give you an indication of the way in which you should work with them.

Actually this power grid is for all project stakeholders and if you end up with a project sponsor that is in the 'low interest' and 'low power' quadrant you really have a problem. It is unlikely that this sponsor is ever going to support your management endeavours.

Types of power that count

Again for all stakeholders, but in particular for project sponsors, you need to be aware that there are a number of types of power that can be present in any organization.

Where does your project sponsor fit?

- Legitimate: This can be through a formal title or position (authority)
- Reward: This can be through an ability to provide positive consequences on people (carrot)
- Coercive: This can be through the ability to provide negative consequences (stick)
- Purse String: This can be through budget control (money)
- Bureaucratic: This can be through knowledge of the 'system' (intelligence)
- Referent: This can be through association with someone else's power (network)
- Technical: This can be through technical knowledge relating to the project (skill)
- Charismatic: This can be through personality alone (character)

Can you categorise your sponsor? Probably they will have more than one of the above lists will apply, and that it a good thing.

Discover what's in it for them?

Finally you need to understand what 'is in it for them' – what their previous experience as a sponsor has been (both in their knowledge of being a sponsor and of real project experience; i.e. was a previous project a nightmare project?) if that is appropriate. Even if they have never 'sponsored' before they will, no doubt, have an opinion based upon stories they have heard from projects in the past.

And 'what's in it for you' is the ability to work in that desired 'Productive Lazy' management style but still deliver for your sponsor.

Manage your sponsor well and they will be you ally in the coming weeks and months.

And now the answer to the question:

A young woman goes to the funeral of her mother. There she meets a man whom she has never met before. She identifies him as the man of her dreams and immediately falls in love with him. She has no idea who he is, and nobody at the funeral has ever met him before or who knows who he is. Two weeks later she kills her sister. Why?

Well, if you think in a very particular way, a way that indicates some potential as a psychopath allegedly, then she killed her sister in the hope that the mysterious stranger at her mother's funeral would also attend the sister's funeral as well since the only connection seems to be with the family and therefore by creating another critical family event, she may well see him again.[2]

Trouble with sponsors

In the book *Strategies for Project Sponsorship*, we offer advice on many types of sponsors with suggestions for ways to work with them or compensate for the 'skill' or 'interest' gaps. We also speak of the concept of the 'balanced sponsor' – being involved in a project, being objective about a project, being supportive of a project. And being reactive to a project's needs.

If you sponsor offers none of the key attributes and remains distant from the project, disengaged and/or uninterested, then first you need to find out the root cause:

- Do they not know how to act as a sponsor?
- Or do they not believe in the project or want to be associated with the project in any way?

Test the reality with a one-on-one with the sponsor. If they are willing to give you their time, then it may mean the problem is the former one in which case:

- Speak honestly about the issues you are facing and the challenges your project is dealing with as a consequence of their lack of involvement
- Discuss what is expected of project sponsors and what the business also expects

If it is the second reason then go back to the business case and explore the original thinking:

- Did they have concerns at the start of the business case – and if so, what were they?
- Or do they see their role as sponsor as a nuisance that is just an added burden to an already business schedule?

Based on this understanding you can plan to mean to re-engage the sponsor if possible, and if not, you need to plan to 'fill the gap' through your own efforts and possible additional executive support.

Notes

1 It does not have to be a woman; gender plays no role in this question or in the answer.
2 I have only come across three people so far who have answered this question correctly (or incorrectly depending upon your view of life). These people each answered almost instantly with the answer above and were amazed that no one else could see the puzzle solution. And, scarily, I am related to one of them!

A project manager's tale where sponsorship was a fast-disappearing commodity

I once attended a meeting, with another experienced colleague, with a group of three individuals in an English company. This company was very interested in initiating a business change project and engaged myself, and colleague, to complete a project readiness assessment.

This assessment was a common service offering that ran over two days and allowed us to consider all of the 'readiness' of any company for a planned for project. We would look at the business case, objectives, and perceived project deliverables. We would consider risks and constraints. We would assess resources and management support for the project. And we would, at the end of the two days of interviews, go away and produce a project success plan outlining the project at a high level and indicating, thorough a 'traffic light' system any areas of weakness in the project. Red issues requiring mandatory action before commencing the project, and amber (orange) issues requiring action as early as possible in the project lifecycle.

So, we turn up day one with the brief to interview 'the three sponsors of this project'. The IT manager, the Sales and Marketing director and the Operations director.

We are greeted by the IT manager, and he laid out the bare bones of the project (this gave us some concerns as this immediately seemed to be an IT rather than business led project, always a challenge). Anyway, we spent two hours with the IT man, and then he took us off to meet the Operations director.

Nice office with a big whiteboard, and up stands my colleague and outlines everything we know about the project to be. Proudly turning to the Operations director, confident in his professional style and ability to absorb and re-present information, he asked if he had 'missed anything'.

'Yes', came the solid reply 'The point!'

It became clear, as the IT manager and the Operations director began to argue – quietly at first and then significantly louder – that there was almost no level of agreement between the two. Indeed, it seemed as if they had never even discussed this before. A red alert on our report was guaranteed.

DOI: 10.4324/9781003506522-26

Eventually we were asked to leave the office and wait. We were shown a small area with a balcony that we could wait in and so, on a fresh Spring morning we stared out over the balcony and waited. And waited. And waited some more.

Eventually we decided to head back to see if any common ground had been established, or perhaps one of the combatants had finished the other one off. But nothing. There was no one to be seen, anywhere.

Confused, we managed to find ourselves back in the reception area and got a call through to the IT manager. Shaken and definitely stirred, he took us to lunch in the café and then pointed us the direction of the Sales and Marketing director.

It was my turn to speak, so I stood up and repeated the position and understanding that we had up to the start of the meeting with Operations director and waited. Waited for a repeat of the last meeting.

'Looks really good', came the response from the Sales and Marketing director.

Naturally we, me in particular, were enormously relieved. We were back on track.

Well we were for all of two minutes!

'That said, I don't really care that much', chuckled the Sales and Marketing director. 'I have just handed in my notice, resigned, so I won't be around'.

So we went from three project sponsors to none in one morning; one because he was leaving, one because he had no belief or support for the proposed project, and one because he was just too weak and non-communicative to act as an effective project sponsor.

In the end it didn't matter that much. We delivered our report as best we could, and the project was never initiated.

Manage the Creep

Watch out, watch out there is a project creep about

It is not malicious, and it is not planned, but the Project Creep is out there and will attempt to, at the very least, confuse your project. The creep may be one person or many; they may have influence and authority or they may not; they may be in your project team or outside the team; they may be your ally and they may not. But what they will try and draw in to the project, that you have so carefully planned, is change.

Project Creep (as in functionality-creep, feature-creep, mission-creep and scope-creep) is a problem where the objectives of the project are put at risk by a gradual increase in overall objectives as the project progresses. So the Project Creep needs to be carefully managed, controlled, anticipated and dealt with.

Change, however, is good, and the one thing you can be sure on any project is that change will occur. So it is not change itself that we should fear but change in an uncontrolled manner and without thorough consideration for all impact and consequences.

So beware the Project Creep. As a wise man once said many years ago: 'Keep your project team close and the project creep closer'.

Well actually, what he really said was: 'Keep your friends close, and your enemies closer' and the 'he' was Sun-Tzu, a Chinese general and military strategist ~400 BCE, and he said it in his book *The Art of War*, but you can see what I am saying, I'm sure.

DOI: 10.4324/9781003506522-27

Applying the 'Productive Lazy' approach

Creep is inevitable

The creep or creeps are out there, and, in their mostly non-malicious way, they just want what is best for the business, which may, or may not, be what is best for the project. Remember, your job is to manage the project and deliver the agreed deliverables. Your job is to control the changes that are raised and support only those that are approved.

In general, the later a change is approved in the project lifecycle, the greater the impact cost will be. Gaps identified early on during the planning phase, through prototyping, or simulation, or any such means, can be evaluated and incorporated with a much lower level of additional investment than changes identified later on.

And here I am not just referring to investments of cost.

DOI: 10.4324/9781003506522-28

Measure the creepiness

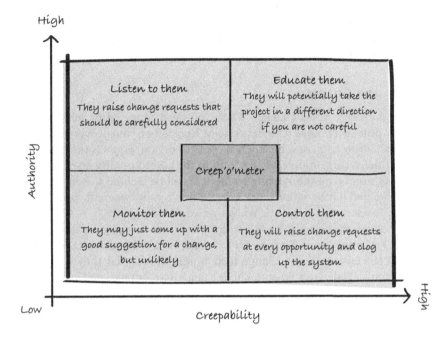

High

Authority

Listen to them
They raise change requests that should be carefully considered

Educate them
They will potentially take the project in a different direction if you are not careful

Creep'o'meter

Monitor them
They may just come up with a good suggestion for a change, but unlikely

Control them
They will raise change requests at every opportunity and clog up the system

Low

High

Creepability

Figure 5.9.1 Creep'o'meter.

Why not see if you can profile your project team and assess the general 'creepiness' of your project.

Use the Creep'o'meter above (yes, another grid) to consider your colleagues and see if you can identify the 'hotspots' for potential creep.

OK, so you have done that, what is the next logical step in the defence against scope creep?

Use the process

You have a change control process, well I hope you have, so make sure that everyone, and I mean everyone, understands what it is, why it is there, and how to apply it. Display it up on the wall of the project office, print it on mouse mats, t-shirts, posters, anything that puts it in front of people as much of the time as possible.

Then, when the very first change comes through, ensure that it goes through the change procedure absolutely, to the letter, without any deviation, and use this case as an example for all on the project to see.

Make it very visible to everyone how this first change request has been managed, where it is in the process, what decisions were taken and when, what is the outcome. Explain also the alternatives that could have occurred – if the change was rejected then what would have happened if it had been approved, and vice versa.

Manage the Change

When is a change not a change? When you have educated people enough that they don't even raise it in the system! Remember your job is to deliver the project, visionary concepts are not yours to dream, yours is the practical reality of delivering on time, at cost, and to the agreed quality level.

Phrases no-one on the steering committee will be pleased to hear include 'OK, we've had a little bit of scope creep. I don't know where it came from, but have you seen this cool little widget we've added...'

The use of more agile[1]-based project methods can also reduce scope creep. A key principle of Scrum[2], for example, is its recognition that during a project the customer can change their minds about what they want and need (often called requirements churn), and that unpredicted challenges cannot be easily addressed in a traditional predictive or planned manner. As a result, Scrum adopts an approach of accepting that the need cannot be fully understood or defined, focusing instead on maximising the team's ability to deliver quickly and responding to emerging requirements.

Park it in the parking lot

A great way to keep people happy to say, 'not now, later on...', it occasionally even works with my kids.

The 'parking lot' is a means to record suggestions and requested changes, or even just ideas, in a place so that they are not forgotten. People will be happier if they know that their 'great idea' has not been forgotten or screwed up and thrown in the wastepaper bin. If they can see you have duly noted and considered their idea and only deferred action until a later date (after this project phase), then they are less likely to complain and cause problems for you.

Park it but don't forget it

But don't forget that 'parking lot', you will have to do something with at the end of the project. I would suggest including all the suggestions as a section of your project closure report. This way, people will see their ideas as valuable contributions, and ones that have been properly managed by the project, by you and by their company. It will then be up to the project steering committee to consider them for a further phase of the project or reject them. The important thing is that this mechanism a) does not discourage people from raising suggested ideas; b) does not turn them against the project; c) does not clog up the change system with unnecessary change requests; and d) removes you from the role of rejecter (if indeed that is the end result).

Thank them, thank them all

And finally, despite the varying levels of 'creepiness' out there, despite what you might feel about the changes themselves, and despite where you are in the project lifecycle, thank each contributor to the change register.

For sure, prepare them for what you expect, educate them in the process and the impact, persuade them to allow you to park their ideas in the 'parking lot' but don't alienate them. They are most likely only trying to help after all.

Notes

1 Agile methodologies generally promote a project management process that encourages frequent inspection and adaptation, a leadership philosophy that encourages teamwork, self-organization and accountability, a set of engineering best practices that allow for rapid delivery of high-quality software, and a business approach that aligns development with customer needs and company goals.

2 Scrum is an iterative incremental process of software development commonly used with agile software development. Despite the fact that "Scrum" is not an acronym, some companies implementing the process have been known to adhere to an all-capital letter expression of the word, i.e. SCRUM. Although Scrum was intended to be for the management of software development projects, it can be used in running software maintenance teams, or as a program management approach.

A project manager's tale of when no doesn't really mean no

The project steering committee was a large one on a project I managed back in my early days of project management. There were, as there are in most projects, some real characters on the committee, and one particular person had a very specific attitude to this project, I was to find out, and a very determined intention.

Yes, it was project commissioned by the company as a whole but, as they had, through their family, a particular connection with the founders of the company, this person felt that they had a special relationship and authority.

Anyway, in the specification work that took place over a three-month period one particular piece of functionality was requested, investigated, reviewed and formally rejected after considered discussion. In general, it was felt that this feature, neat though it may well be, was not crucial to the overall success of the project and was overwhelmingly wanted by the intended users. And, as far as I was concerned, that was that. Move on.

And move on we did; the project was well underway when I happened to be in the rest area enjoying a coffee and some peace and quiet when the 'character' sat down opposite me.

'How's that work coming along on my request?', he asked.

Well, I was at first confused but after some further conversation it began to become clear that he was talking about his 'pet' requirement, the one that the steering committee had rejected. It was as if he had never been at any of those specification review meetings, never received or read any of the change communication and certainly wasn't in the meeting when this particular request was rejected.

I explained the situation once more.

'Shame' was the only reply I received as I was left alone at the table with my coffee once again.

I put the conversation down to just confusion on the other person's part and quickly forgot about it. I may, in fact, have rapidly moved my attention on to a nice piece of chocolate cake that I was enjoying with my coffee.

DOI: 10.4324/9781003506522-29

At the next steering meeting I had a moment of déjà vu, when the two of us, in the period before the meeting proper had started, had an almost identical conversation. The only difference was that the 'Shame' response was appended with an 'It would really help us if we had that, pity' comment.

Patiently I explained the situation once more.

That, sadly, was not to the end of it.

A similar thing happened over the next 18 months at irregular intervals. Conversations would be struck, outside of meetings, at the coffee machine, in the car park, on the way through reception, but it was never confrontational and never aggressive. It was always polite and with a sort of sad and wistful conclusion when each time I responded in the same way, 'Shame'.

It was like the goldfish in the goldfish bowl with the three-second memory span[1]. 'Ooh look a castle', swim, swim, swim, 'ooh look a castle', swim, swim, swim 'ooh look …' – you get the idea.

Patiently each time I explained the history, the process and the decision. Each time I would get the same response, more or less, 'Shame'.

Finally, we reached acceptance testing and sign off by the steering committee.

Despite all of the formalities of the process that were in place, despite the signed specifications stored away, despite the contract locked away in legal, and despite all of my best efforts, approval was delayed until the 'special feature' that was so much wanted by my colleague was duly re-costed, developed, tested and accepted.

How did this happen? What did I do wrong?

Well for one thing, I was outmanoeuvred, the person in question managed to get the role of acceptance manager, and that gave them a position of added power, and second the same person had influence at the top that they utilised to get their own way, influence that outranked that of the project convention. I was also fooled by their calm demeanour, apparent patient acceptance each time I explained the position and apparent (repetitive) acceptance of what I was telling them.

They were a very special sub-set of the 'high authority – high creepability' group focused on the one special change that seemed to them so important. Not to the business as a whole but personally to them.

I was never going to win this one, but perhaps I should have re-registered the change request and taken it a second time through the process and in front of the steering committee. I will never know. Perhaps if the attitude had been different, argumentative and demanding, then the situation may well have been dealt with much earlier. But it wasn't.

The project creep comes in all shapes and sizes, so beware.

Note

1 Yes, I know, Goldfish don't have a three second memory span. Research by the School of Psychology at the University of Plymouth in 2003 demonstrated that goldfish have a memory-span of at least three months and can distinguish between different shapes, colours and sounds. They were trained to push a lever to earn a food reward; when the lever was fixed to work only for an hour a day, the fish soon learned to activate it at the correct time.

Risky business

Surprises are not welcome here

The buttered cat paradox is a common joke based on the tongue-in-cheek combination of two pieces of wisdom:

The first is that cats always land on their feet.

And the second is that buttered toast always lands buttered side down.

Now consider what would happen if the piece of buttered toast was attached, butter-side up of course, to the back of a cat and then the cat was dropped from a large height.

Some people suggest that the following will occur. As the cat falls towards the ground, it will slow down and start to rotate, eventually reaching a steady state of hovering a short distance from the ground while rotating at high speed as both the buttered side of the toast and the cat's feet attempt to land on the ground.

This idea appeared on the British panel game QI, where as well as talking about the idea, they also brought up other questions regarding the paradox. These included 'Would it still work if you used margarine?', 'Would it still work if you used I Can't Believe It's Not Butter?', and 'What if the toast was covered in something that was not butter, but the cat thought it was butter?', the idea being that it would act like a placebo.

The supposed phenomenon of the buttered toast reaction was first observed in the *New-York Monthly Magazine*, which published the following poem in 1835:

I never had a slice of bread,
Particularly large and wide,
That did not fall upon the floor,
And always on the buttered side!

A study by the BBC's television series Q.E.D. found that when toast is thrown in the air, it lands butter-side down just one-half of the time

DOI: 10.4324/9781003506522-30

(as would be predicted by chance)] However, several scientific studies have proven that when toast is dropped from a table it does fall butter-side down at least 62 per cent of the time.

Why is this? Well, when toast falls out of a hand, it does so at an angle. The toast then rotates. Given that tables are usually between two to six feet, there is enough time for the toast to rotate about one-half of a turn, and so it lands upside down relative to its original position. Since the original position is butter-side up, then the toast lands butter-side down.

Now ignoring the paradox and concentrating on the simple piece of buttered toast dropping from your hand, you could address this 'risk' in two ways. The first being that you rip out all of your kitchen fixings and tables and then re-install new ones that are at least 10 feet off the ground. This will result in any future toast drops have a 50/50 chance of turning sufficiently to end up buttered side up – a saving of 12 per cent of cases using the Q.E.D. experiment results. But this would be pretty costly and impractical.

Alternatively, you could just be more careful when you eat buttered toast. Sit down. Don't rush. Have the butter and toast on the table together. This would potentially deliver greater end results, providing a significant reduction in dropped buttered toast in the first instance and therefore the percentage of cases where the toast falls buttered side down would be irrelevant.

Risk management needs to be relevant, appropriate and reasonable.

Besides, cats hate having toast stuck to their backs!

Applying the 'Productive Lazy' approach

Change is risky

It has to be accepted that all change is risky.

Presumably this change, this project that you are leading, has more than reasonable advantages for gain that significantly outweigh the cost and the risk., and so, the project manager, have the task of considering these risks and deciding what you will or might do about them.

If you are running an IT upgrade project, reasonable risk might be that the SME (subject matter expert) you have in-house could fall ill or be unavailable for some reason. The way of addressing this risk therefore might be to use external expertise (just in case). An unreasonable risk might be that a meteor could hit the western hemisphere and cause multi-country mayhem and general chaos. Leave this one off the list, because a) it is so remotely unlikely to happen that it isn't worth the effort; and b) what on earth would you do anyway? Presumably the IT upgrade would put on hold or become completely irrelevant.

Think risk

One of the most useful actions I have seen occur at the end of a project is the process of both lessons learned (we will talk about this later on in the book) but also lessons shared with regards to risk.

This is a scaling challenge normally; yes, there is a ton of data and experience at the end of the project but how do you share it with others outside of the project.

If we flip to the other end of the project – the start – we all know what goes on, don't we?

OK, new project – great! Must do a risk assessment and build a risk mitigation plan but I am so busy.

OK – now looking at my last project which is not dissimilar to this one then I can simply cut and paste and hey presto – risk planning done. Next.

DOI: 10.4324/9781003506522-31

I know I would never ever do this, and nor would you.
Of course not.

Right project manager, right risk

At a higher level, the overall risk to a project needs to be considered and assessed.

There is a strong argument for profiling both projects and project managers in order to match them appropriately – I mean, if you have a high-risk project, why would you blindly assign a less experienced project manager? Makes no sense.

This risk profile needs to be weighted according to each organisation but should, at the end of completion, provide a clear picture of the overall risk to the organisation if this project is approved (obviously against this will be the strategic need and the anticipated benefits).

The key here is 'no surprises' – if this is one scary hairy beast of a project, then let everyone involved know that it is just that and be prepared.

Mapping against this project profiling should be a project manager profile or capability equivalent. It needs to answer the question: is this project manager suitable, capable and experienced enough to handle this particular project?

Let's say that an organisation simple categorises their projects in to three profiles; simple, difficult and complex (however they decide to do that).

Now if that same organisation has 20 project managers, we need to be honest and accept that those 20 project managers will not have equal experience, skills or competence. And so this organisation profiles their project managers into three levels: Junior Project Manager, Project Manager and Senior Project Manager.

These three project management levels should map to the project profile categorisations to make real sense.

And so if the organisation initiates a complex project, then there is no logic in putting a Junior Project Manager in charge as they will only have sufficient proven experience to manage a Simple project. Putting them in charge must add to the overall risk of that project.

Now logic says that for a complex level project, the organisation's duty is to appoint a Senior Project Manager.

It is possible, in order to develop project management skills and gain experience, that say a Project Manager (mid-level) is appointed to support a Senior Project Manager on a complex (third level) project, or even manages a complex project under the guidance of a Senior Project Manager and so on.

Be honest in your own capability and don't chase projects beyond your capability without some help and guidance[1].

Each organisation must define both the project and the project management profiles and make sure that they align. They must further have a process to support and develop project managers from level to level to create the future 'complex' project capable project managers.

A new risk

In recent years there has been a rise in projects utilising resources and covering user communities that span countries and continents alike, resulting in the rise in numbers of project managers who have to manage not just local but also international/remote teams. Add to that the inevitable rise of low-cost offshore resources that many IT projects utilise on a regular basis, then even a 'local' project can have a global aspect to it.

Such teams face many additional challenges. Consider the added dimensions of time and of distance in the global world, the impact of language in communication, the demands of appreciating and respecting varying cultures, of working with resources that may abide by alternative allegiances, and finally the complexity of multi-country regulatory discipline.

All of which adds up to even more of a challenge for the project manager – and failure is not an option these days either, as those projects that are commissioned are deemed ever more critical to the business strategy and therefore success.

Working, as will be most often the case in 'international' projects, in a matrix environment makes these issues so much worse where the resources that the project needs are shared among more than one project and priorities are often defined by the local functional manager. Here the dimension of allegiance comes in to play very strongly and, for those resources that a project manager has secured but who are perhaps challenged by the project work or have a personal preference for their own local work, he dimensions of time and distance can create a great barrier to hide behind. The results being that project work is neglected, but the resource remains locally respected, owing to the other work that they are completing through their line management.

Note

1 Your PMO might well be the place to get this sort of help and guidance.

A project managers tale of practical risks

Working with one organisation I was delighted when they considered risk management and that they thought like this.

Lessons learned are good and this will share perhaps 80% of the knowledge amongst team members – each team member will move on to their next project wiser and better prepared – and this is a good thing.

But, being a realistic organisation, they also thought that outside of the project team the majority of project managers would not have the time or the inclination to actively and thoroughly share the knowledge to the full project management community – nor did they have a tool that would help this happen, so they decided to go for the most important piece of information or knowledge that should result in the greatest impact on their future projects.

Realising the real limitations of how to share the knowledge that they had, and the nature of the majority of the project managers, then this organisation asked the project community to name one thing that would help them the most in this area. The response was loud and clear. Risk.

They mandated that one lesson learned was to be recorded and shared at the end of the project. They noted what the biggest and most unexpected and most impactful issue was and what action was taken to deal with this issue.

In essence, what was the most unwanted surprise and how did they handle it?

This knowledge was updated regularly and inserted into their in-house methodology tool and was, as a result, both used and updated (because project managers saw and experienced the value).

Simple but effective.

DOI: 10.4324/9781003506522-32

5.14

Communication Breakdown

Avoiding having a nervous breakdown and going insane[1].

Good communication is comprised of more than how the message is delivered. The information itself, the method used, and the timing with which it is delivered all contributes to effective communication.

- Right information
- Right time
- Right person
- Right way

Communication on a project is a two-way process. You are communicating out, and you are receiving communication back at you, and the usual complexities of filters and noise typically confuse the process of giving and receiving clear, accurate and understandable information.

Communication is also sequential, communicated through chains of people, which will add that 'Chinese whispers' effect – either intentional or accidental.

Add to that the sheer volume of communication these days, email, phone calls (landline and mobile), written, presented, verbal and so on, then life can be very tough for project managers to learn what they need to learn and to share what they need to share.

I was taught a truth in my early project management days – reporting is not communicating! The fact that the critical facts and important truths are buried somewhere in a report that the right people may be in possession of does not, in any way, mean that they have received the message.

I have also learnt that to waste time and effort in 'defensive' and 'offensive' communication, typically email these days, is truly pointless and will distract the project manager from the real issues. I know building an email trail that, to put it bluntly, 'covers your ass' is easy to do but far better results can come from directing those same efforts in really effective communication.

DOI: 10.4324/9781003506522-33

Effective communication is about isolating the critical information, utilising the optimum communication method for the person (or people) that you need to communicate with and delivering that information at the appropriate time. I would also add that to ensure that you receive the right information back to you, then you need to educate people on what information you need, how you would like to receive that information and when.

Note

1 Led Zeppelin were an English rock band formed in London in 1968. The group comprised vocalist Robert Plant, guitarist Jimmy Page, bassist and keyboardist John Paul Jones and drummer John Bonham. Communication Breakdown is one of the author's favourite songs.

Being Erediginous

I used to encourage project managers the world over to adopt the word 'ticketyboo[1]' as this can describe a project status with strength but vagueness all at the same time.

I know – bad communication (but sometimes useful in my own experience in confusing people or buying time).

But now I have progressed on to 'erediginous', a much grander word that covers just about anything (if you ever run out of words).

Erediginous (adjective)

Definition:

- Originating from the need to describe the indescribable but also the relevant to any conversation or argument
- Exhibiting a quality or action or position that is difficult to define but has meaning in the moment

Usage:

- "He was being particularly erediginous today"
- "She welcomed them all to this most erediginous event"
- "The project manager was incredibly erediginous"

But why, you may ask?

Well, 'erediginous' is a term coined to describe something that's difficult to define but still relevant or meaningful in a given context. It's a concept, sort of like a placeholder for describing things that defy easy categorisation but still hold significance.

And that can apply to many things in project management and beyond.

Go forth and be most erediginous.

DOI: 10.4324/9781003506522-34

Note

1 Tickety-boo, an informal adjective meaning "fine, OK" is a British colloquialism of uncertain etymology. It may be an expressive alteration of "that's the ticket," ticket here having its informal sense "the proper thing, advisable thing". Or tickety-boo may be a holdover from the Raj, from Hindi *ṭhīk hai* "It's all right", or *ṭhīk hai, bābū* "It's all right, Sir". Tickety-boo entered the English language in the first half of the 20th century.

Applying the 'Productive Lazy' approach

'If you wish to persuade me, you must think my thoughts, feel my feelings, and speak my words' Cicero[1], Roman orator and statesman, once said.

Communicate as others need you to communicate

This whole book is really about communication, but this chapter covers communication in specific. And the lazy project manager will think very, very carefully about what they need to communicate and how they need to communicate it and why they are communicating what they are communicating.

The general guidance is that some 70 per cent of a project manager's time will be spent in communicating. 70 per cent!

So, if you play the productive lazy game at all, and you only apply it in one area of project management it makes blinding sense to do it here, in communication. This is by far the biggest activity and offers the greatest opportunity of time in the comfy chair.

Imagine if you would be able to save some of that 70 per cent of your time, how much more relaxed would you be?

Understand how communication works

Now, you can go and do your homework, you can read a book, you can attend a course, you can 'Google' to your heart's content, and you will find lots and lots and lots of information about communication[2]. I really don't want to get too technical here, but simply put, and just so that you have a basic understanding, here is a summary:

There is a source: someone/something sending out the information.

There is the medium: this is the means by which the information is sent. Maybe this is spoken or electronic (email, message, workflow alert etc) or through the telephone. Maybe it is paper-based (letter, poster, memo, Post-it, etc), or it could be an image or visual or a sound. It can actually be silent

DOI: 10.4324/9781003506522-35

through a look, a smell, body language, colours or the arrangement of text (numbers or letters).

OK, then we have what is known as the receiver: someone/something that is receiving the information...

And the final part of the process is feedback: the source will not know whether the communication that has been sent has been successfully received unless some feedback is received (some action or change in behaviour).

OK, got that, easy, eh? Well, no, there is a little more (well lots more if you study the topic properly):

Communication is just not simple, there are lots of different types of medium by which to send information, and the way that the receiver understands the information might be very different to that which was intended. Most of us will have received a text message from someone that was taken to mean something completely different from what was intended. For example, the same can applied to email.

On top of all that, there are actually barriers to communication that can add to the challenge of communicating in successful and clear way. These can include:

- Language (you are communicating between speakers of different languages or, if in the same language there may be an imbalance in the level of those language skills, or local dialects may be in place)
- Content (maybe there is some 'deep space' technical content involved or acronyms or just long words that not everyone understands. Another variant of this are the levels of knowledge and expertise of the sender and the receiver)
- Understanding or the lack of understanding of what the receiver wants or needs (how they wish to be communicated with and what they want to communicated)
- Feedback (there can be a level of inadequate feedback, or none at all – have you ever been on those long conference calls where nobody says anything apart from the speaker?)
- Emotional – your very mood can cause communication interference (if you are angry or upset)
- Quality of the information being sent
- The medium used (resigning from your job by text is not advised, for example)
- Lack of trust or honesty in the source
- Lack of attention from the receiver (maybe a matter of priority, the status of the source or just poor listening skills)
- Cultural differences

There are so many, that it is amazing that we can communicate as well as we do on a daily basis.

Well, often I failed at this. For example, telling my three boys when they were younger it is time for bed should be easy. "Adam, Sam, Scott, time for bed" – job done. In reality, they will be watching the TV or on their laptops or playing their game machines or more typically doing all three at the same time. I will be somewhere else in the house, and they won't be listening anyway, and even if they did, they would be filtering me out, because they don't want to hear this particular piece of information. And so it results in the message being sent many times, at varying ranges and volume (and accompanied by increasing threats/incentives).

Be honest and be open

So having solved all the above challenges on communication, I would suggest that in order to keep the levels of successful and productive communication high, then it is very important that you are both honest and open in all of your communications. Even if you cannot share everything with others, you can at least be open and say that that is the situation and why.

Be honest and keep your promises, do what you say you are going to do, deliver what you say you are going to deliver. Trust is critical. The lack of trust or honesty in the source (you) is, as we have already seen, one of the barriers to communication. But if you fail someone, then they are not only likely to resist future communications; they are less tolerant about understanding such communications.

And finally, honesty in communication should also extend to not over-promising or 'overselling' anything.

There is very good Swedish saying "Sälj inte skinnet förrän Björnen är skjuten", which roughly translated means 'Do not sell the skin before the bear is shot'[3].

What is the point in successfully communicating to someone and overcoming all of the challenges that that entails, only to communicate something that isn't even true?

Communicate in the modern way

Welcome to the era of digital communication, where emails and texts have evolved into Zoom calls and Teams messages, where mobile phones and BlackBerrys have been replaced by smartphones and tablets. In this fast-paced world of virtual meetings and instant messaging, shouldn't communication be easier than ever before?

Well, yes and no. The reduction in face-to-face interaction, replaced by emails, texts and virtual meetings, has its drawbacks. Misunderstandings are more common when visual cues are absent. We've even developed shorthand like emojis to compensate for this loss. Additionally, the sheer volume of communication has skyrocketed, and inboxes are overflowing daily. Furthermore, the rapid pace of technological advancement often means that less time is spent crafting thoughtful messages.

Here are some modern tips for effective and efficient communication in the digital age:

- Adapt Your Communication Style: Just as you adjust your tone and style in emails, tailor your approach to suit each individual's preference, whether it's a quick Teams message or a scheduled Zoom call.
- Communicate Your Preferences: Let others know how you prefer to be contacted and why. Whether it's via Teams chat for urgent matters or email for formal documentation, clarity is key.
- Set Communication Priorities: With the deluge of messages, prioritise who and what you respond to, ensuring critical information gets immediate attention.
- Seek Feedback: Confirm that your messages are understood by the recipient. For important matters, consider following up with a quick Teams call to clarify any confusion.
- Delegate Strategically: Utilise your project team on platforms like Teams to delegate tasks and streamline communication, freeing up your time for essential matters.
- Filter and Delegate: Don't get bogged down in unnecessary conversations. Filter out non-essential messages and delegate tasks whenever possible.
- Empower Others: Encourage team members to take ownership of communication tasks when appropriate, fostering a collaborative environment on platforms like Teams.
- Embrace Self-Resolution: Encourage problem-solving within teams before escalating issues, utilising platforms like Teams for group discussions and resolutions.
- Avoid Overcommitment: Before diving into a conversation, ask yourself if it's necessary and if you're the right person to be involved. Respect your time and that of others on platforms like Teams.
- Master Digital Efficiency: In the realm of Outlook and email, prioritise essential messages, summarise lengthy threads and keep your inbox clutter-free for better focus. Remember, concise messages lead to clearer communication.

In conclusion, while modern communication tools like Zoom and Teams offer convenience and efficiency, effective communication still requires thoughtful consideration and strategic use of available resources. So, embrace these tips to navigate the digital landscape with ease and productivity.

Reporting is not communicating

Every project should have a communication plan in place. Make sure that everyone knows what this plan is and how they should be contributing to it.

Also, validate its effectiveness on a regular basis, if it needs amending do so – and let everyone know.

Another well-known project management law, Cohn's law, sums this up so well. 'The more time you spend in reporting on what you are doing, the less time you have to do anything. Stability is achieved when you spend all your time doing nothing but reporting on the nothing you are doing'.

Putting together fantastically accurate and detailed reports and sending them to anyone and everyone, is most definitely not communicating. They won't be read, no one has the time or interest to do this, and they won't be valued and worse, when they do contain project critical information, they will be ignored. You are wasting your time. And, yes, AI is providing a whole new way of 'communicating' through automated production of meetings notes and minutes.

Notes

1 An accomplished poet, philosopher, rhetorician and humourist, Marcus Tullius Cicero (106 BCE–43 BCE) was also the greatest forensic orator Rome ever produced. But to Cicero, service to the *res publica* (literally, 'the public affair') was a Roman citizen's highest duty.
2 Communication is the process whereby information is imparted by a sender to a receiver via a medium. Communication requires that all parties have an area of communicative commonality. There are auditory means, such as speaking, singing and sometimes tone of voice, and non-verbal, physical means, such as body language, sign language, paralanguage, touch, eye contact or the use of writing. Communication is defined as a process by which we assign and convey meaning in an attempt to create shared understanding. This process requires a vast repertoire of skills in intrapersonal and interpersonal processing, listening, observing, speaking, questioning, analysing and evaluating.
3 At least that is what they tell me it means; knowing the Swedes, it is probably more likely to be something odd that involves snow and sex. If so, then you have my apologies for inadvertently offending you. In this case it is best to just use the English translation. However, if the translation is correct, then the Swedes have my apologies: lovely people, and great snow.

A project manager's tale of the perils of coffee machine communication

Working for a Japanese company, I assumed the project management role some four months into the project, there was another project manager before me, a colleague, who had decided to 'move on'.

Being a diligent and conscientious project manager I sat down with the team and reviewed the plan and the schedule.

It became rapidly clear that the project was going to be late, and instead of a 'go live' date of 1st February it was more likely that a 'go live' date of 1 May was achievable.

Anticipating the discussion, I was going to have to have with the customer's project manager first, and then the steering committee later, I dutifully researched and documented the reasons behind the slippage of three months.

In all honesty, they were 95 per cent down to the customer. What my predecessor had failed to do was to communicate these slippages in an appropriate way. I could find all the causes and consequences buried deep down in the copious project status reports (each one an average of 12 pages long!), but none of this had risen to the surface at recent project meetings or steering meetings, and therefore this was going to be a bit of a shock.

So, fully prepared for my meeting later with the customer, I needed to head off to see another customer just down the road. As I left, I commented to my technical architect that I was off, would be back 3 pm, and 'would give the bad news then'.

I left. I returned.

The first person I met on my return was my technical architect, who cheerfully informed me that he had met the customer project manager at the coffee machine earlier and gave him the news.

And the result? Well, I had a tough meeting, and I never got the opportunity to present the facts of the situation and build up to the consequences in a proper manner. I was on the back foot from the moment I walked in the door and never recovered. I was also replaced on the project in a few weeks,

DOI: 10.4324/9781003506522-36

and the third project manager assumed control and delivered the project (on 1 May).

Our sins: We had failed to communicate from the start of the project in an appropriate way, and when there was bad news, we communicated in an inappropriate and casual manner without control or consideration. My failure was that I did not communicate well enough to my project team what I intended to do and why I wanted to do it this way, nor the potential consequences of not being able to do it this way.

Chapter 6

Productivity – Journey

Personal success is a multifaceted journey, defined by both long-term aspirations and immediate actions. At this point we delve into the intricacies of defining personal success at two levels: the grand vision for the future and the practical steps for immediate change, whilst emphasising the importance of setting multiple goals across various aspects of life, from career to relationships, and achieving a balanced fulfilment. It encourages introspection into one's current state and desires, urging readers to list what they want and what they don't want, setting the stage for meaningful change.

Central to the discussion is the concept of saying 'no' more often, a key aspect of productive laziness. Critical to this we explore the psychology behind reluctance to refuse, offering insights into overcoming the fear of confrontation and prioritising personal needs. Additionally, providing practical strategies for effective decision-making, such as assessing urgency and considering alternative approaches.

DOI: 10.4324/9781003506522-37

Personal Success

Defining your personal success can be done at two levels. You could go for the big 'where do I want to be in life in say five or ten years' time approach and the 'what are my goals in life' approach.

Answering those questions will give you a long-term plan for your personal destination of choice.

Or you can answer at a lower level with the 'what things do I do that I could easily change that might make a real difference' and 'what is it that I do now that I know I shouldn't do' approach. This will at least point you in the right direction of the changes that would bring about a significant difference over time and an immediate difference quickly.

Personally I am always a fan of the 'quick win' approach. It delivers fast and it fuels the feeling of success and the momentum of achievement.

We all want to succeed in more than just one area in our lives, so you do need to set multiple goals. For example, one goal may relate to your career and work while other goals may relate to your relationship, children, or hobbies. You need to ask yourself 'What kind of balance do I need in my life?' And you must find a balance between all these areas of your life in order for you to feel fulfilled.

So where are you now? What is your starting point for change?

The greater clarity you have in defining your 'journey' the more likely you are to succeed, or to put it another way – the less chance you have of getting lost on the way. The other great benefit of seeing the full journey is that you can plot your simple steps and not be put off by a belief that any change is just way too enormous and far too difficult to achieve (so why bother trying).

I am with Confucius when he said, 'A journey of a thousand miles begins with a single step.' And I like to make those first steps very small ones if I can.

What does 'success' mean to you?

DOI: 10.4324/9781003506522-38

The easiest thing to do is to start with what you know:

- Do you know what you want?
- Do you know what you don't want?

For example you might think 'I want to spend more time with my family, but I don't want to do a bad job at work and not have a career in project management'. This is perfectly acceptable and aligns itself to the guidance of having balance in what you do.

It is possible that you don't know what you want, or even worse, you don't know what you don't want.

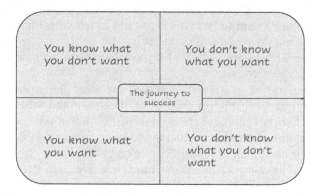

Figure 6.1.1 The journey to success.

The journey to success can only be plotted once you have a clear route mapped out.

Part of this, in the interest of not wasting time and effort, is in avoiding the things that you don't want and focusing on the things that you do want. It is a little like going for a walk. There are two types of walks: the 'A' to 'B' type where the purpose is to get to 'B' from a starting point of 'A'. And there is the second type where you have plenty of time and the pleasure in the walk is to take your time and discover interesting places on the way. For a 'productive but lazy' person the 'A' to 'B' journey is the one to go for – in fact a truly 'productively lazy' approach would look at whether you could in fact miss 'B' out altogether and go straight to 'C', if 'C' is your next destination.

Let's start with your journey now.

Can you now list everything that you believe you do want and would like to change? Honesty is really important here – just put it down on paper or electronically, your choice, but put it down somewhere.

What about the things that you know you don't want? Can you list these as well?

Take some time now to do this, trust me, it is definitely worth the effort (even if you are a rushed off your feet, always busy, never have any spare time sort of project manager).

1. What do you want?
2. What don't you want?

Yes, I know that first list is going to be a whole lot easier to put together than the second one, but the more you understand about yourself and what you want the better.

Great, now we move on to the other part of the journey.

Now, can you think about how you would find out about the things that you might well want if only you knew what they were?

Talking to other people often helps here – widening your scope of knowledge and experience through others (we will look at your network of influence later on).

What about the things that you don't know that you don't want?

Well perhaps all you can do here is anticipate that, as you progress along your path to change, you will probably stray into this area once or twice so be ready. If it doesn't feel right, then challenge it.

This is not a one-time only self-assessment – you will need to re-test yourself with the questions of need and desire several times over as your journey progresses.

The Power of No, the Strength of Yes

Just say No

Making a productively lazy list is all well and good but one of the real consequences of doing this and changing the way that you are going to work in the future, will be the need for (and of course the benefit of) saying 'no' a whole lot more often.

Most of us know that we really should say 'no' a little more often than we do, but for some reason it is difficult to utter the necessary noise that would deliver this decision.

And yet, in contrast, my kids seemed to have absolutely no problem with saying it many times each day. When we are tiny, it seems the only word we can utter is 'no' as we try to assert ourselves in the big wide world, but as we get older, we tend to feel guilty when we have to say 'no' to other people. We regularly give in because we just can't stand the thought of upsetting others, being seen as 'mean', or just don't want to make a fuss.

There is another factor I believe. If you say 'yes' then the conversation is pretty much over. The other person might start to explain in detail what you need to do to complete the thing that you have just agreed to do but for you, the apparent effort is over.

Now on the other hand, saying 'no' will most likely require you to immediately put in some additional effort in justifying why you have said 'no' and why you can't, don't want to, shouldn't do it, etc. A 'yes' equates to less effort now (but a whole lot more later), while a 'no' equates to effort right now, up front, immediately (but conversely a lot less later on).

But saying 'no' can actually be a good thing for all involved and can definitely be a good thing for you.

Well it's not '50 ways to leave your lover[1]' but more 'fifty ways to leave something alone that you are better off not getting involved in'. To aid your capability in responding in the negative here are some helpful words, in case you have forgotten them 😊:

DOI: 10.4324/9781003506522-39

1. Nie – Afrikaans
2. Jo – Albanian
3. La – Arabic
4. Nie – Belarusian
5. Na – Bengali
6. Ne – Bulgarian
7. No – Catalan
8. Bù – Chinese
9. Non – Creole (Haiti)
10. No – Croatian
11. Ne – Czech
12. Ikke – Danish
13. Geen – Dutch
14. No – English
15. Ei – Estonian
16. Ei – Finnish
17. Non – French
18. Ara – Georgian
19. Nein – German
20. Ókhi – Greek
21. Lo – Hebrew (Israel)
22. Nahi – Hindi
23. Nem – Hungarian
24. Nei – Icelandic
25. Tidak – Indonesian
26. No – Italian
27. Wa – Japanese
28. Aniyo – Korean
29. Ne – Latvian
30. Néra – Lithuanian
31. Ne – Macedonian
32. Tidak – Malay
33. Ma – Maltese
34. Ikke – Norwegian
35. Na - Persian (Farsi)
36. Nie – Polish
37. Não – Portuguese
38. Nu – Romanian
39. Niet – Russian
40. Nema – Serbian
41. Ne – Slovak
42. Brez – Slovenian
43. No – Spanish

44. Hakuna – Swahili
45. Ingen – Swedish
46. Mïmi – Thai
47. Yok – Turkish
48. Nei – Ukrainian
49. Không – Vietnamese
50. Nid oes – Welsh

Now here is something interesting. Out of all those languages the longest word for 'no' is six letters, the shortest is two letters, and the average is three letters. So again, why is it such a difficult word to say? I mean there are much tougher words to enunciate – such as 'pneumonoultramicroscopicsilicovolcanoconiosis[2]'.

If you find that one easy, try:

'Llanfairpwllgwyngyllgogerychwyrndrobwllllantysiliogogogoch', which is a large village and community on the island of Anglesey in Wales, situated on the Menai Strait next to the Britannia Bridge and across the strait from Bangor. The village is best known for its name, the longest place name in Europe, and one of the longest place names in the world[3].

Either way, you have to admit 'no' is a lot simpler.

When someone asks you to do something you really don't want to do you need to learn to say 'no' – simply 'no'. You don't have to avoid replying, apologise or make up excuses, in fact making up excuses tends only to make matters worse over time. You just need to say it clearly and firmly. After all, it is your choice.

In many cases, not saying 'no' becomes one of the greatest challenges to our own productivity. What happens in these situations is that we place the satisfaction of others ahead of our own.

Why on earth do we do this when most likely we do know better?

Well there are many different reasons:

•   We want to help other people. Some supposedly positive behaviours are confused with other supposedly negative behaviours. Refusing to do something is considered to be a selfish act, while accepting something is seen as a non-selfish act, both altruistic and generous.
•   We fear rejection by other people. We all want to be liked by others, therefore we seek their approval, often at a cost to ourselves.
•   We fear losing potential opportunities from other people. We believe that if we say 'no' now then well, in the future we won't be offered other interesting opportunities.
•   We respect other people. Sometimes we feel that another person just doesn't deserve a 'no' response from us.
•   We experience guilt when we don't help other people. We are often quite worried after saying 'no', even if it is the right and proper thing to do. Human nature leads us to feel concerned.

And perhaps the most common one:

• We are fearful of confrontation with other people. We want to avoid unnecessary conflict and maintain a good and happy atmosphere.

All of these are indeed reasons that we find saying 'no' difficult, but none of
them is good reasons to not say 'no'. Try to resolve to say 'no' more often. It
won't hurt you – honestly – and it won't hurt other people either if you are
sensible and sensitive.

Prioritise your valuable time and don't be persuaded to waste it just to
please someone else.

It doesn't mean you are being selfish, but sometimes you do need to put
your own needs first.

You might say 'no' for a good reason other than the fact that you don't
want to do it or need to do it. You might, for example, say 'no' because there
is a much better qualified person who could do the job in a far more effective
way in a shorter time than you could.

The principle here is that allocating work to the best-suited person benefits everyone in the long run. Of course this cannot be done just to avoid
work. You have to pick up some actions yourself otherwise you will never
achieve anything. And there is the 'what goes around comes around' idea as
well. Sometimes you shouldn't say 'no' because despite the fact that you may
not want to do something, need to do something and there is someone who
could do it better, you do want to help out and be that team player or Good
Samaritan.

Or it is in your interests to take on a project so you can learn some new
skills, in which case you may well not be the most obvious person for the
job.

It is all about balance and priority. Overall you want to deal with the
important stuff plus a reasonable amount of other stuff.

If you keep saying 'yes', then your backlog will never go down and you
will spend far too much time working on the unimportant.

Just say Yes

What happens when you do say 'yes'?

We have had the 'fifty ways to say no' so why not 'five ways to say yes'
(well I do want to encourage you to say 'no' more often than you say 'yes'):

1. If I have to
2. OK
3. Good
4. Great
5. What are we waiting for?

'If I have to' isn't such a great way to get on board and won't win you many friends or influence people. It smacks of an attitude and a reluctance that shouldn't be there. If you have done all of your prework and considered all of the relevant questions – need, desire, appropriate person, duty – then you are going to do it, so why not do it with a smile and with enthusiasm. It may well turn out to be one of the 'I don't know what I do want' situations and you might have fun. Either way if you do the task well and happily then 'what goes around comes around' may well benefit you later on in life.

'OK' is, well, OK. You are on board and will no doubt do the best that you can.

'Good' takes a step up the ladder of enthusiasm and a 'great' sounds like you will put everything you have into the business of successfully completing the work to the best of your ability.

Best of all is 'What are we waiting for' as this shows that not only will you put 100% effort behind this and do a super job, but you will also most likely take the lead as you clearly strongly feel both that this needs to be done and done by you.

But 'yes' can be less 'black and white', it can also be a subtle shade of grey. In a very good way.

Just say Maybe

This is the concept of 'ATP[4]', which stands for 'available to promise'. It is used a lot in manufacturing and sales but simply put it means that you can say 'yes' but then qualify that with a consideration of what it is that you can promise someone now, tomorrow, next week or next month. If the work needs doing and you are signed up for it (somewhere between a 'if I have to' and a 'what are we waiting for'), then can you do more if you wait a while?

Can you do even more if you wait a little while longer?

When you agree to do something think carefully about the real urgency and the potential benefit of holding back for a while.

You might do a much better piece of work if you didn't rush in right now and that might be beneficial to everyone rather than an 'OK' delivery now. Talk to the recipient of your planned efforts and explain that they could say, have a little now, a little more fairly quickly, but if they want the whole then they would have to wait a bit longer.

Say 'no' firmly – say 'yes' when a 'yes' is appropriate – say 'how much and how soon' openly – and be clear in all that you say and do.

And beware the double positive!

A linguistics professor was lecturing to her class one day. 'In English,' she said, A double negative forms a positive[5].

A voice from the back of the room piped up, 'Yeah, right.'

Lazy success

There are a number of questions that you should ask yourself:

- Do I want to do this piece of work, job or task? Even if I do want to do it, do I need to do it?
- Is the result or outcome worth my effort?
- Do I have to do it myself?
- If I have to do it then what is the shortest path to the point of success?
- What exactly is that point of success and at what stage will I just be wasting my time?

What we will do now is work our way through these questions and challenge, at each step, your current thinking and behaviour.

Want and need.

We have seen that the reason you should be doing this is that your efforts should be focused on the 20 per cent that matters, at least to begin with, and the only way you can do this is to assess each task or job as it is placed in front of you. Your 'to do' list needs to be sharp, focused and definitely relevant to what you are trying to achieve.

The starting point should be the 'do I want to' and the 'do I need to' questions. Always ask them together in order to come up with the right answer.

Is there a compelling reason for doing a task or not? If not, then don't do it.

If the answer formulates as a 'yes', then it may be time to move ahead.

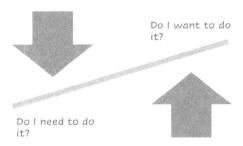

Do I want to do it?

Do I need to do it?

Figure 6.2.1 Need and want.

The second stage after the 'want' and 'need' evaluation is the consideration of whether the outcome expected is worth the anticipated effort.

These elements evaluate the 20 per cent and we then consider the likely outcome.

With three 'yeses' in the bag, it is still not a done deal just yet.

Consider now whether, even though you want to do something, you really are the right person to actually carry out the task. Is there someone better qualified who can and will do a better and perhaps faster job than you?

If there is why are you thinking about doing it?

Focus on the important stuff.

Having allowed yourself some time to think about what it is that you should focus on and therefore also allowed yourself the benefit of doing some simple planning, you can focus on the important stuff, as opposed to worrying about the less important stuff.

You have asked the first three important questions and now the buck really does rest with you because you are committed, you are taking ownership of this one.

But even now the 'less is more' mantra should be sounding in your mind.

When you do get on to doing the things that you should do then consider this:

- Can you automate it? Can you scale it? Can you make it reusable in a wider context? Use that creativity that you have, that all productively lazy people have, and make 'it' repeatable, suitable for a wider purpose and audience, easily available without you having to act as a gatekeeper all the time (thereby taking up your time).
- Can you simplify it? Can you shorten it? If there's something that you do that is complicated and difficult, find ways to make it easier and simpler. List the steps and see which can be eliminated or streamlined. Which steps can be done by someone else or automated or dropped completely? What is absolutely the easiest way to do this?
- Can it wait? Is it really needed when it is supposed to be needed? Will it impact on others if it waits? Sometimes, not always you understand, but just sometimes, not rushing into something can turn out to be a productively good thing as it turns out it didn't matter anyway, or at least the need has gone away. We live in a complex butterfly and hurricane world of interaction[6], so at any given time just about everything is changing.

At every opportunity you must think your actions through to the end, as best that you can, and aim to optimize your personal return on your personal investment.

If all of this sounds rather cold and clinical, even cynical in some cases, it really isn't. It should be second nature to all of us to consider each request, to promise only what we can realistically deliver, and to be honest with ourselves about what we want in life.

After all you are on a journey to productive laziness powered by personal productivity, aren't you?

Notes

1 '50 Ways to Leave Your Lover' was a 1975 hit song by Paul Simon, from his album Still Crazy After All These Years. '50 Ways to Leave Your Lover' broke in the US in late December 1975, becoming No. 1 in the US Billboard Hot 100 on 7 February 1976 and remaining there for three weeks. It was certified gold on 11 March 1976 and remained a best-seller for nearly five months. The song also topped the adult contemporary chart for two weeks. It remains Simon's biggest solo hit.

2 An obscure term ostensibly referring to a lung disease caused by silica dust, sometimes cited as one of the longest words in the English language (45 letters in total).

3 We will discover a new word 'erediginous' later in the book – a word that will be most useful in learning, I would suggest.

4 Available to promise (ATP) is a business function that provides a response to customer order enquiries, based on resource availability. It generates available quantities of the requested product, and delivery due dates. Items can be promised to customer order requirements for a given period based on an uncommitted or available status, calculated as: on-hand inventory, less booked customer orders, plus expected master schedule receipts for the period.

5 A double negative occurs when two forms of negation are used in the same clause. In most logics and some languages, double negatives cancel one another and produce an affirmative. In other languages, doubled negatives intensify the negation. The rhetorical term for this effect, when it leads to an understated affirmation, is litotes. In some languages, though, such as Russian, a double negative is still a negative. However, there is no language wherein a double positive can form a negative.'.

6 'When a butterfly flutters its wings in one part of the world, it can eventually cause a hurricane in another' Edward Lorenz, pioneer of Chaos Theory. 'Butterflies and Hurricanes' is also a song by Muse from their third album, Absolution, and was the last single released from the album. It was one of two songs recorded with a string section, both of which were recorded, along with an early version of 'Apocalypse Please', during the initial stages of recording. The song is notable for its Rachmaninoffesque piano interlude. The song concerns itself with the so-called butterfly effect of Chaos Theory, describing how even tiny changes in present conditions, like the flap of a butterfly's wing, can cause big differences in the future.

Chapter 7

Laziness – Much, Much Thinner in the Middle

In this middle part, we emphasise the role of the project manager in fostering a fun and enjoyable atmosphere within the team, utilising humour and team bonding activities to alleviate tensions and enhance collective productivity. By promoting a culture of controlled relaxation, the project manager encourages team members to handle challenges with composure while maintaining a sense of camaraderie and enthusiasm for the project's goals.

It is noted that for a good project manager the skill of staying calm in the face of crises is key, and we will see parallels to this in the advice given during emergencies on flights.

Through effective planning, delegation and prioritisation, the project manager can navigate unexpected challenges with clarity and efficiency, ensuring that the project remains on track. By fostering strong team dynamics and empowering team members to take ownership of their responsibilities, the project manager strikes a balance between accessibility and control, allowing the project to progress smoothly while conserving energy for critical interventions.

DOI: 10.4324/9781003506522-40

Driving the project from the comfy chair

The Lazy Project Manager's Theory of Projects, from a Productive Laziness aspect:

"All projects are thick at one end, much, much thinner in the middle and then thick again at the far end".

The 'lazy' project manager now oversees the project work with as light a touch as possible. The planning was done at the 'thick' front-end of the project, now it is all about execution and control.

A number of aspects work well in the world of productive laziness – first ensuring that the project is conducted in a fun and enjoyable manner, and second being prepared to throw that book down or stop surfing the internet, leap off of the comfy chair and deal with problems as and when they occur but in a controlled and productive manner.

In addition, it is always good to spread a little love across your project team to engender good spirits and a confident air of potential success. Such love is a good thing, but you do need to avoid the trap of being swamped with attention, you need to learn how to operate an 'open door' policy but avoid getting dragged in to every little project detail.

'A whole is that which has beginning, middle and end' Aristotle[1].

Note

1 Aristotle (384–322 BCE) was an Ancient Greek philosopher and polymath. His writings cover a broad range of subjects spanning the natural sciences, philosophy, linguistics, economics, politics, psychology and the arts. As the founder of the Peripatetic school of philosophy in the Lyceum in Athens, he began the wider Aristotelian tradition that followed, which set the groundwork for the development of modern science.

DOI: 10.4324/9781003506522-41

All in a Fun Day's Work

Taking it all a little less seriously can be good for your project health.

"I love deadlines. I love the whooshing noise they make as they go by".

Douglas Adams[1]

You have to laugh; well, I think you have to laugh.

Without a little bit of fun in every project, then the project world can be a dark and depressing place.

Setting a professional but fun structure for your project can really be beneficial for when the problems start to rise to challenge your plan of perfectness. And problems will inevitably arise.

In the years I have done many things to encourage team bonding, lighten the darker moments of project hell and defuse difficult project-related situations. I have even accepted the full and complete blame for every problem, issue and challenge to a project in front of a room full of project team members, before walking outside and firing myself (in a loud voice; well, voices – one mine and one me pretending to be my boss). The net result was a diffused situation, where it had previously been extremely confrontational between teams and individuals.

Done well, this does not damage your status or authority but can actually be a very positive act in people seeing you a human being, and not just a project manager, and thereafter wanting to share a smile and a laugh with you during the day.

It is just the same in that hotbed of confrontation, the home!

Try looking at one of your children when they are in a really bad mood. Look them in the eye, with a serious face, and point a finger at them and say'Don't laugh! Don't you dare laugh! If you laugh you will go straight to the naughty stair!'. I bet at the very least you will get a smile out of them.

You will find that, even in the most stressed out, aggressive, emotional and 'in your face' moments, if you can make the opposition (and I use that term loosely) laugh then the war is soon over.

DOI: 10.4324/9781003506522-42

It is hard to kill someone when you are laughing[2].

Well, I guess that is true except for some of the more extreme psychopathic[3] types ("No, I expect you to die, Mr Bond[4]" ... cue maniacal laughter).

Notes

1 Douglas Noel Adams (1952–2001) was an English author, humourist, and screenwriter, best known for The Hitchhiker's Guide to the Galaxy. Originally a 1978 BBC radio comedy, The Hitchhiker's Guide to the Galaxy developed into a 'trilogy' of five books that sold more than 15 million copies in his lifetime. It was further developed into a television series, several stage plays, comics, a video game and a 2005 feature film.
2 Check out *The Project Manager who smiled* by Peter Taylor for lots more fun and fun inspiration.
3 And you already know how to spot those people don't you.
4 A copy of the famous James Bond scene with Goldfinger.

Applying the 'Productive Lazy' approach

Start with a smile and a joke

A Project Manager and her principal architect and her chief analyst were having a lunch time stroll along the beach, as you do, when they happened upon a small brass lamp lying on the sand. Eagerly they grabbed the lamp and rubbed it and, of course, as in every fairytale, the giant genie appeared in a puff of magic smoke.

"I am the genie of the lamp", he proclaimed "and I will grant you three wishes".

He paused, as if noting for the first time that there were in fact three people staring at him.

"As there are three of you then you will have to share the traditional three wishes. Each of you will be granted one wish each. Who's first?", he asked.

The ever-eager principal architect did not hesitate a second. "I wish that I was on a tropical island with sun, sand, clear blue water and palm trees, oh and with a group of nubile girls delivering endless cocktails".

"No problem", said the Genie, and with a quick flash and a puff of smoke, the architect disappeared.

"Wow", said the chief analyst "I wish I was in fast and expensive sports car driving through the mountains to my magnificent villa overlooking the Mediterranean, where I will drink champagne and eat caviar".

"Easy", said the Genie, and with another quick flash and another puff of smoke the analyst disappeared as well.

"And what is your wish?", commanded the genie to the project manager.

"Simple", she replied, "I want those other two back at their desks by 1:30 prompt!".

Make fun part of your project

We all know about the team phases, 'forming – storming – norming – performing – mourning'[1] – if you don't, there is plenty of information on the topic out there in 'Google-land'.

DOI: 10.4324/9781003506522-43

Now I would suggest that to have a little bit of fun can really help calm the nerves during the storming phase when team conflict and competition can be high; it should be indoctrinated into the norming phase as the team develops their working rules and processes; and finally, during the performing phase I am convinced of the value of fun in keeping the team at peak performance.

Here's a few ideas:

Working with a colleague we used to put 'secret' fun messages in presentations that we each gave. This allowed us to have a laugh or two, and in fact challenged us to put more and more difficult words and phrases into business presentations without anyone else spotting something odd was going on. I extended this to a full project team once. No one knew that the others were in the 'game', everybody thought it was just them and me. It was very amusing. The meeting had a great feeling about it, everyone was happy and smiling. And yes, it was very productive.

You can do things like 'It's Friday' the one day of the week when the team care share 'funnies' through email[2]. This is good because it limits to a degree such emails to one day of the week and it should also make the team consider what is appropriate for general sharing rather than just sharing everything.

One team I led all enjoyed many happy moments, once a year, when we 'talk like a pirate' on, honestly, 'Talk like a Pirate' day'[3]. Check it out.

And my current Global PMO[4] team love having fun. We have a lot and, guess what, we are hyper productive as a result (you can check out the book we wrote together for all the amazing fun ideas we have had 'Projects: Methods: Outcomes – The New PMO Model for True Project and Change Success'[5].

And here is my favourite 'ice breaker':

Place the group you have in to small teams of 4 or 5 ideally, anymore and it gets a little difficult.

A flipchart or whiteboard is needed for each team (or at least a piece of flipchart sheet).

Get one person in each team to draw a large circle in the middle of each sheet and then draw a line out from that circle for each member of the team (so team of four = four lines).

Now ask the teams to discuss among themselves and identify:

• Three things that they have in common
• One thing that is unique to them

Allow them five minutes to do this, and try to guide them away from really easy things like football, beer, work, shopping, etc.

Allow ten minutes for this and when everyone is done get the groups to remain standing and ask one person from each team explain the team's results – for fun, see if the other teams can guess the unique things.

This process a) avoids the creeping death introductions around the table; and b) gets the group relaxed and knowing a little more about each other, it is surprising what you will find out about your colleagues in a very short time that you didn't know before. I guarantee the results will be the topic of conversation at the next coffee break.

Practice safe fun

Obviously, it has to be acceptable fun – don't want to be 'PC' here, but do be careful – think carefully about your team members: does your idea of fun equal other people's fun?

Also bear in mind there are times to have fun and times to be serious, you and your team must understand the parameters of this. And there may be members of the project team who just don't want to have fun, make sure that they are not excluded or isolated from the rest of the team.

Make you fun smart fun

Now, when you have this whole 'work hard but have some fun' project underway the smart, and by that I of course mean 'productively lazy' project managers, will sit back in the comfy chair, and let their project team self-generate the fun working atmosphere.

Done right, you will have set the acceptable parameters for fun in your project, both in content and in extent, and you will have engendered that spirit amongst your project team to the point where, one day, when you are the one on a low, they will make come up and make you smile.

End with a laugh and a wave

A man in a hot air balloon was lost. He reduced altitude and spotted another woman below. He descended a little bit more and shouted:

"Excuse me madam, can you help? I promised a friend I would meet him an hour ago, but I don't know where I am".

The man replied: "You are in a hot air balloon hovering approximately 30 feet above alkali desert scrub habitat, 2.7 miles west of the Colorado River near one of the remnant populations and spawning grounds of the razorback sucker".

"You must be a biologist", said the balloonist.

"I am", replied the woman. "How did you know?"

"Well", answered the balloonist "everything you told me is technically correct, but I have no idea what to make of your information, and the fact is I am still lost. Frankly, you've not been much help so far".

The woman below responded, "You must be a project manager".

"I am", replied the balloonist "but how did you know?"

"Well", said the woman "you don't know where you are or where you're going. You have risen to where you are due to a large quantity of hot air. You made a promise to someone that you have no idea how to keep, and you expect me to solve your problem. The fact is, you are in exactly the same position you were in before we met, but somehow it's now my fault!"

Have fun on your projects.

"And no Mr Bond, I expect you to laugh".

Notes

1 The Forming – Storming – Norming – Performing model of group development was first proposed by Bruce Tuckman in 1965, who maintained that these phases are all necessary and inevitable in order for the team to grow, to face up to challenges, to tackle problems, to find solutions, to plan work, and to deliver results. This model has become the basis for subsequent models of group development and team dynamics and a management theory frequently used to describe the behaviour of existing teams. Tuckman later added a fifth phase – Adjourning – that involves completing the task and breaking up the team. Others call it the phase for mourning.

2 Check any policies that your company may have regarding non-business emails.

3 This is not a joke, it is a real 'International Day'. www.talklikeapirate.com/piratehome.html. Have fun 'talking' like a pirate, using email 'translators' to create pirate speech communication, and even slap on an eye patch and a parrot to get in to the mood. Just for the one day, you understand; any more than that and you are probably just odd.

4 Shout out to Bill Snow, Kim DiMauro, Thomas Neumeier, Brandy Kirsch, Ahmad Jamal, Kathy Rousseau, Sally MacQueen, Erika Williams, Lauren Shankle, Jost Lange, Jason LaPrade, Matt Parker, Mitch Rajmoolie, Leanne Falcon and Lila Thakoor.

5 www.routledge.com/Projects-Methods-Outcomes-The-New-PMO-Model-for-True-Project-and-Change-Success/Taylor/p/book/9781032387307.

A project manager's tale of self-humiliation

There was a time when I cared what others thought about me but that time has mostly passed, I still care a little, of course.

I think a significant turning point came a few years ago, not too many years ago come to think of it when I was working on a global programme within my own company. The programme was simple in its concept – develop a standard project management methodology, train everybody in that methodology and then make sure that everyone used the methodology all of the time.

Parts one and two (develop and train) were not without their challenges but were achieved within 12 months, which was pretty good going. Part three proved to be the really difficult part. We met with not resistance as such but more apathy and a general mood of "just smile politely and they will eventually leave us alone to carry on as we have always done". Adoption rates were low, and we were failing.

We had many (many) discussions, workshops, conference calls, brainstorming sessions and the like to try and work out what could be done to drive adoption that much faster. And all these ideas pretty much fell in to two camps – the incentive category (or carrot) and the punishment category (stick).

One aspect of working on a global project was that conference calls, among the team, were often held at unusually early or late calls, and on one of these late long calls I had finally had enough.

As the conversation went around and around the carrot and stick, stick and carrot, all carrot and no stick, all stick and no carrot options, I suddenly stated, "What we actually need is the Giant Killer Carrot of Death".

Silence.

Laughter.

"Oh we'd pay to see that", came the general response, and so, two weeks later, and having secured a suitable costume I was outside my house having my photograph taken in a giant bright orange and green carrot costume (I was very surprised when I contacted a large fancy dress costume hirers

DOI: 10.4324/9781003506522-44

and requested a vegetable outfit. They listed a quite impressive list of options of both the vegetable and fruit variety).

And so it came to pass that the 'Giant Killer Carrot of Death' began his (do carrots have a gender?) reign of driving adoption in the methodology.

I really don't think that the whole root vegetable thing helped in any way with the future adoption levels of the methodology, but it certainly made the team laugh and gave them all a great introduction to many conversations, meetings and presentations after that (with the highest 'laugh' factor being the ones where they did this when I was also in the room):

"Have you seen Peter dressed as a carrot?"[1]

I like to think I made a few people's working day a little lighter.

It was all in day's fun, that's for sure.[2]

Notes

1 Photographs can be obtained, one free with every 500 copies of *The Lazy Winning Project Manager* purchased.

2 I was more than happy to 'take one for the team' in this way.

Breathing Normally

The benefits of staying calm in a crisis.

You are on yet another flight, either to or from your latest project engagement, somewhere in the world. Maybe you have been lucky, maybe the flight is on time, and you know your luggage is safely stored in the overhead locker, you are not seated in the middle seat between two sumo wrestlers with body odour and this flight does offer complimentary in-flight beverages.

You settle back in your seat and begin to drift into that 'yet another flight' snooze, vaguely aware that the air hostess is, for the one thousandth time, explaining to you how to complete that complex conundrum of buckling and unbuckling your seat belt. You begin to disengage from the world around you...

But wait! The flight crew in the uniform, vainly talking to everyone but knowing no-one is listening in return, is about to utter a supreme piece of wisdom.

In the event of an emergency, an oxygen mask will drop in front of you from the panel above. Place the mask over your mouth and nose, straighten out the strap, and pull the strap to be sure it is tight on your face. After you are wearing it securely, a tug on the hose will start the oxygen flow. It makes sense to put your own mask on first, before helping others. Breathe normally.

Breathe normally.

To begin with, I used to think that this was the craziest thing possible to say. If I was ever on a flight where the oxygen masks were to drop down, you can be sure that I would place the mask over my face, pull the strap as tight as possible, tug the hose until I felt the sweet taste of oxygen flowing. But the last thing I would do would be to breathe normally. I would breathe like it was my last moments on this earth (or air at this point, earth presumably about to enter the equation in a rather nasty crashing, crushing, exploding sort of way).

Breathe normally.

Not a hope in hell!

DOI: 10.4324/9781003506522-45

But actually breathing normally is really, really good advice. Being calm, wasting less energy, wasting less oxygen, thinking clearly and considering the situation in a reasonable, objective manner is absolutely what is most likely to help you to survive.

In the project world, when all around you are going crazy with panic (and that may well include the sponsor), breathing normally will allow you to consider the situation, assess the core issues, plan a response and carry out the actions with the minimum amount of effort and to the maximum effect.

Applying the 'Productive Lazy' approach

Stay calm in a crisis

So to begin with you must stay calm in a crisis, really, this is most important.

The majority of potential critical situations that you may well face in a project should have, in fact, already been considered as part of your risk planning and mitigation activity[1]. If you have done a complete and proper job at the start of the project (you remember, that point in time when even the productively lazy put in a solid day's work to get the project in the right shape to begin with) then you should have at hand plans of action for the majority of crisis you are likely to face. Each eventuality should have been considered, reviewed, discussed, planned and have a conceptually proven response defined by yourself and your project team.

Plan for the crisis

If so, then for these situations you have at your fingertips a menu of actions that will mitigate or at least reduce the issues you are facing. No need to panic there then.

That will still leave a small percentage of situations that you either did not consider as part of your risk strategy plan (if so, this will be a learning exercise for you for future projects) or really have blind-sided you because of their completely unexpected nature. Maybe the 'Big Red Bus' that is so often joked about really has caused mayhem for you?

Breathe normally

Begin by counting to ten – seriously, try it. There is something in the human nature that says when there is a major issue identified that action is instantly required to resolve it. In reality, a short calming moment will allow a better chance of considering the issue in a more complete manner, and this in turn

DOI: 10.4324/9781003506522-46

will result in a decision of action that is more likely to address both the issue at hand and any associated consequences. The last thing you want to do is put out one fire only to start another one somewhere else, one that could be worse than the first one.

Equally, there is something else in human nature that can lead us to that 'rabbit in the headlights' state – that is frozen in complete inactivity by the oncoming crisis. With the project team looking to you to decide and set the required recovery plan in to action, you do .... nothing.

Breathe normally.

You need to be in control, and you need to make the right decision, so look after yourself first – 'It makes sense to put your own mask on first, before helping others' – and once you are ready to consider your response to the problem then you should filter – filter – filter.

Filter, filter, filter

Identify the issue or issues and the source of those issues and filter out those that either do not require you to resolve them or indeed are better resolved by others on the team. Nothing in the rule book says the project manager is the best person to deal with every issue, every crisis, and every threat to the project's success. Quite the opposite is true in fact. Don't try to be the project hero all of the time, it is not your job and the move from hero to zero comes damn fast!

Once you have filtered the issue or issues then take the next step which is to delegate – delegate – delegate. You have a project team for a good reason, so use them, use the breadth of their skills and knowledge to help you and the project overcome whatever is causing the problem.

Delegate, delegate, delegate

Remember while a problem shared is a problem halved, a problem delegated is a problem not on your plate right now, thereby leaving you free to get on with your real job, consider all implications of any recommended actions and oversee the project being steered back to safety. Hurrah!

Your one true job is to Breathe normally.

Applying the 'Productive Lazy' rule, I would personally aim for 80 per cent of the issues being solved by others and maybe 20 per cent of them being solved by you, or at least with you leading the resolution. You still don't have to do it all on your own.

So, you have filtered (filtered, filtered) and you have delegated (delegated, delegated) and now what you need to do is to prioritise – prioritise – prioritise!

Prioritise, prioritise, prioritise

Even those issues that do end up on your plate may not need immediate and urgent action – maybe you have an issue coming at you but right now it is not showing signs of 'clear and present danger'. If so, you have even more time to think and consider before you act.

Deal with the ones that you have to and monitor the others that you don't have to deal with just right now. For those who can wait a little while, maybe you can consider options of action that are open to you and the team ready for future action. Gather insight from you team members and any other source of knowledge that you can reach out to and continue to do that single most important thing.

Breathe normally.

Note

1 Risk management is activity directed towards the assessing, mitigating (to an acceptable level) and monitoring of risks. In some cases, the acceptable risk may be near zero. Risks can come from accidents, natural causes and disasters as well as deliberate attacks from an adversary.

A project manager's tale of enduring the perfect storm

At the height of a particular project and working with a particularly demanding team of people, the project I was managing some years ago hit a problem.

Now the problem was, initially, undefined, the cause unknown, but the effects were quite worrying.

Let me paint the picture a little more. There was a deadline, a quite aggressive deadline, and there was steering committee, a quite aggressive steering committee. There was also a project sponsor of course, an extremely demanding, loud, opinionated, driven individual who I was convinced never actually wanted to see this particular project succeed (quite an unusual project sponsorship position but one which I was sure they had taken).

Anyway, the deadline loomed towards us on the project team, and the technical challenges seemed never-ending. As quickly as one was resolved, another (if not more) seemed to take its place.

The working days got longer, and the toll of all this pressure began to cause serious stress faults in the project team. Their ability to work together became fragile, shall we say. The slightest thing had people at my desk or on the phone complaining.

So, in the midst of all this fractious harmony, we hit the problem. I won't go into the details of the actual problem itself – it was technical and complicated to understand but not complicated to resolve, it turned out.

Now, if the team had been at full efficiency and working as one, I am sure we would have spotted the cause earlier and resolved the issue quickly and quietly. As it was, we didn't do either of them. The cause went unresolved, and the effects seemed to spiral ever towards being out of control completely.

Rapid response meetings were convened, but all the team seemed to do was argue and point fingers of blame at each other as well as at any and every other part of the organisation.

There was a whole bunch of problem-solving techniques attempted and no doubt some real out-of-the-box, blue sky thinking applied without success.

DOI: 10.4324/9781003506522-47

Everybody was trying to resolve this issue. Some even headed to the pub to try and find a cure there; such dedication should be admired.

Anyway, the result? Well, the result was a whole bunch of 'headless chickens' running around the place, and each and every one of them just stopped doing their day job. This resulted in further delays threatening the project and put ever increasing pressure on the poor project manager (me), who had to provide updates to the steering committee and project sponsor. A less than relaxing experience.

Just when I honestly thought it was all going to implode, I had one of those 'eureka' moments. I can't say it was planned, and I can't say it was done in a positive or creative spirit. It was, if I am completely honest, done in a moment when I just lost my temper.

I ordered various parts of my project team off to various parts of the company offices to 'go and do their jobs and get us back on track'. Inadvertently I gave a number of people the authority to stop worrying about 'the problem' and to concentrate once more on their scheduled tasks. In addition to this, and once again I can claim no real skill in orchestrating this, I was left with one fairly junior technical guy and, for the want of anything else to do, told him to head off to the IT department and find someone who could help think this problem through.

And what did I do? Well, I was the one who went to the pub. I admit it, I just needed to escape the pressure and think. I had fallen into the trap of becoming subjective in all the chaos and panic, and I now know I should have remained above everything and objective in my view.

What happened then were three things.

First, I had a very nice steak pie, chips and peas with a pint of beer. Second, the junior technical guy just so happened to talk to the right person; in fact the right person was a combination of the right person inside the company and, purely by chance at that point, the right person visiting from another part of the company. And third, the issue was initially worked around and later resolved through some third-party intervention.

I was lucky, the crisis passed, and the project staggered on for a while and eventually delivered, later than expected, but nevertheless it did deliver.

But it did teach me an important lesson – filter what you should deal with, delegate everything you can, prioritise what is left and then focus on what is important. In this case, I did none of these things and was lucky to get the result that I did.

Giving good feedback

A necessary step to improvement

Some time ago I was in town, and a major sweet manufacturer was handing out samples of its new product, free and with no ongoing commitment, and so it was proving very popular with the shoppers.

It was a sweet that I did like, but it was one of those special limited-edition variants to the standard offering. Personally, it wasn't to my taste; the kids loved it, but for me it just didn't work, and so that was that. I didn't ask for my money back (it was free), and I didn't go and tell them I didn't like it (I just won't buy any of that flavour, although the original is still as good as ever), and I certainly didn't go and complain to the manufacturers about their product.

There is a trend among publishers, and authors (including me) are implicit in this of course, to produce free eBooks. These books are either a free complete book given away in order to hopefully attract new readers to an author for their other books, or a sample of a book (or two) put together to do the same thing: attract in readers who might then buy the full book – at a price, of course.

I continue to enjoy the experience of being an author, but the whole 'being in the public domain' and 'being open to direct feedback' is still a tough one.

I once read *The Tiny Fork Diet* by Alan Sugar[1], which is a promo for his *The Way I See* it book, and I also downloaded Karren Brady's[2] *10 Rules for Success*, in turn a promo for her book *Strong Woman*. Neither was great, but I did buy Alan Sugar's book afterwards. My money, my choice.

Now I have a free eBook called *The Art of Laziness*, and it is a sampler, a freebie to get you hooked – it tries to sell my other books: like, *The Lazy Project Manager*.

For all my books I get reviews, good and not so good – you can't please everyone, of course. But for *The Art of Laziness*, with some 10,000 downloads around the world, I seem to get only bad reviews. Actually, when I

DOI: 10.4324/9781003506522-48

think about it, I would not ever expect a good review or a bad review or any review really, as this is just a sampler of a fuller piece of work. This is not the work that should be judged; that should be reserved for the complete book.

The most recent one was, "A complete waste of time – you have been told, do not download this free book" – it went on, "An exercise in stating the obvious as an apparent advert for his other books. I was hoping to learn something from this, but just wasted my valuable time reading it".

Why do I care, especially as my books sell in the thousands around the world?

Well, it is the cold bluntness of the feedback that stings, I guess, and the inability to respond in any real manner. I politely read all reviews, and I politely thank people for taking the time to post a review and that is that. No chance for a good old conversation about what I was trying to achieve and learn more about why the reader was disappointed. Actually, to be fair, on two occasions the reviewer has responded, and we have chatted about the book, and on one occasion the reviewer upgraded the review by a star or two. On this occasion I was amused that I got two stars for a book that was 'a waste of time', so it could have been worse, I guess!

There may be times when you have to talk to someone in your team about something that they have done, or not done, that has caused the project problems. You will have to give them feedback.

Feedback is hard but essential for us all to improve. I recently got a free coffee. I had collected those loyalty stamps and after buying five coffees I was entitled to a free one. It was horrible, but I was in the car, driving down the motorway by the time I tasted the coffee. At first, I thought, 'This was free, so dump it and forget it', but then I thought – 'Feedback: I should give feedback to help the coffee company improve their product'. And so I did. When I got home, I found the website and submitted a comment. After three days I received the reply "We thank you for your comment about your recent experience with our coffee. We are sorry that you did not enjoy the product this time but appreciate that you are a regular customer and feel sure that your next experience will be back to our usual standard".

The difference?

Well, I read my feedback, and I care about what people say, it makes me feel good sometimes and sometimes it makes me feel bad, but I always care. And the coffee company … well what do you think?

A tough process

Giving and receiving feedback, no matter how well intentioned it is, can be a tough process.

So how do you go about it in a sensitive and positive manner?

Start with the basics then make sure all such feedback is:

- Done in private
- Honest and respectful
- Non-judgmental
- Provided in simple terms
- Provided in easily manageable portions
- Relevant and appropriate at the time

Begin by setting the scene and providing some insight by explaining the problem, the consequences and perhaps suggesting an alternative behaviour that would be better for the future.

Notes

1 Alan Michael Sugar, Baron Sugar, is a British business magnate, media personality, author, politician and political adviser. In 1968 he started what would later become his largest business venture, consumer electronics company Amstrad.
2 Karren Rita Brady, Baroness Brady CBE, is a British business executive and television personality. She is a former managing director of Birmingham City FC, current vice-chairman of West Ham United FC, and an aide to Alan Sugar on The Apprentice.

Applying the 'Productive Lazy' approach

Always address the problem and not the person

Try to make your feedback a joint analysis of the problem, which is typically much easier for the recipient to accept. In my case the free sweet I tasted in town was not to my taste but the only investment I had made was in eating some of it and then throwing it away, I had no feedback to give (maybe the company would have liked some, I'm not sure).

In the case of the book reviews, the investment was not one of financial cost, since the book was free, but yes, there was the investment in reading time to account for.

But looking at the list of basic rules for feedback you can see why this doesn't work with book reviews:

- Done in private: book reviews are done in the full glare of the public domain
- Honest and respectful: generally this is true
- Non-judgmental: definitely not. Many are judgmental, in fact the more they dislike the book, the more judgmental they get, it seems
- Provided in simple terms: sometimes yes. There is always the one-to-five-star measurement, but the supporting words can be simple or complex
- Provided in easily manageable portions: true, one book, one review
- Relevant and appropriate at the time: well, yes, true in a fashion, but I still get book reviews years after the book was published. After all, not everyone reads it the day it is released, and they just come at you out of the blue with no warning

And it is almost impossible to take the review in an objective way; it is your book, and therefore anyone who doesn't like it can't like you, the author.

So it is personal!

DOI: 10.4324/9781003506522-49

Be realistic

A feedback session should ideally cover no more than two issues, since any more than that and you risk the person feeling attacked with the result of them ending up feeling demoralised.

You should also stick to behaviours the person can actually change or influence, so be realistic in what you are aiming to guide the person to change from and to. It can't be an impossible challenge.

Ensure that the feedback is not only negative but begins and ends on a positive – we call this the 'feedback sandwich'. Starting off with something positive helps put the person at ease and lets them see what success looks like. Then you can deal with the issues you wish to cover – not more than two, remember. By ending with some positive feedback, you help them avoid a feeling of despondency and bolster their confidence in order to deal with any negatives.

A project manager's tale of terminal feedback

Many, many years ago I took over a position in a company reporting to a head of department who had been in that position (I worked this out eventually) all of my life.

He had joined this particular company long before I was even a hint of a glint in the spark of a thought in my parents' minds and had eventually risen to a position he was in when I joined the company as a green and eager 'newbie', fresh from college.

He seemed to take a liking to me and assured me that, given time, effort and focus I could achieve similar heights to himself. And so he 'took me under his wing'.

Unfortunately what this meant was that he gave me feedback at each and every opportunity that we were together, in meetings, in one-to-ones, at the coffee machine, in the corridor and once, unexpectedly, and most certainly unwantedly, at the lunch table when I was sitting with some of my peers.

As I look back at this, I realised that the majority of this 'feedback' was critical and negative because I did not do things the exact same way that he did them, even though I was not him and, in my mind, a creative sort of person who aimed to do things the most efficient way.

Sadly the result of all of this feedback, most of which (I can now note) broke pretty much all of the rules – not in private, very judgmental, badly timed, too detailed, mostly negative – was not what he was expecting. I am sure he expected me to be grateful and learn the right way (his way) and one day perhaps even replace him.

For me, the process was too painful and left me feeling disconnected to the role and, if I am honest, pretty down about the whole thing, and so I moved department as soon as an opportunity arose. I wasn't anywhere close to starting my career as a project manager then, but I do remember that when I finally led my first project team and there was a need for some feedback, I instantly recalled this personal experience.

DOI: 10.4324/9781003506522-50

As a result, I went out of my way to ensure that the project team feedback I gave was delivered in the very best way I could at that time – I definitely didn't want my team members feeling the same way I had done all of those years ago.

Perhaps these were early signs of future productive laziness showing through.

A lot of 'Lurve' in the Room

It's a team thing!

It's not about you. No, really it isn't.

Well that's a truth but there are many and varied ways of working with teams, leading teams, managing teams, and getting the very best out teams. People, as well you know, are immensely complicated things.

Your approach may well vary depending upon the nature of project management in the organisation that you are working in. Is this a 'one-off' or are you likely to have some of the team members on your next project. Is the project driven for the greater good of all or is this a business change critical project where people are expendable? It is a jungle out there sometimes and only you and your sponsor will know the need of your projects. Some projects will allow for people development, and some will not.

You can read and learn from many sources on the means of assessing team members, characterising them, identify optimum working partnerships and working styles, and generally getting the best out of the team as a whole. Equally you can read about driving teams to the very 'edge of chaos' where a team can actually deliver magnificent productivity, but with a limited and potentially fatal 'shelf life' for those in the team.

So many choices but, as a general rule, consider this – a little love goes a long way, and a lot of love goes much further. Consider your team, care for your team, love your team, but you don't have to marry them.

Remember: the relationship isn't forever. It is just for the lifetime of the project – but then of course there is always the next project, so you never know.

Going virtual

Transitioning to a virtual work environment opens up a world of possibilities for enhancing remote productivity. Yet, it's not without its unique challenges. Collaborating across continents, bridging cultural gaps and navigating

DOI: 10.4324/9781003506522-51

different time zones are just a few hurdles virtual project teams face. However, with the right approach, the benefits of this global connectivity are vast and ever-expanding.

At the heart of successful virtual collaboration lies executive sponsorship. Management's genuine commitment to embracing virtual work, backed by adequate technological support and training, is paramount. Merely granting permission for remote work isn't enough; proactive support is essential for teams to thrive in this setting. Reflecting on my own journey, transitioning from office to remote work involved a steep learning curve. I quickly realised the importance of discipline and guidance to adapt effectively.

While communication technologies facilitate virtual teamwork, there's no substitute for face-to-face interaction. Ideally, team members should meet in person or engage in one-on-one conversations to humanise their relationships. Relying solely on conference calls or webinars, Zoom and Teams etc risks creating impersonal communication channels. But embracing such tools using their fast-extending capabilities for messaging, chat, collaboration, whiteboarding and more can help recreate the spontaneous exchanges typical of a physical workspace.

Key is to never forget that you are dealing with people – other humans, just like you (or at least similar to you).

Establishing a sense of camaraderie and shared purpose is crucial in virtual projects. Despite physical distances, teams must align their objectives to drive collective progress. Embracing diversity becomes a strength, enriching the project with varied perspectives and experiences. The project manager plays a pivotal role in fostering knowledge sharing, cultural understanding, and deep engagement within the team.

Ultimately, embracing the virtual project world requires a blend of foresight, adaptability, and proactive support. With the right strategies in place, teams can harness the full potential of remote collaboration while nurturing a sense of unity and purpose across boundaries.

Applying the 'Productive Lazy' approach

Make your project attractive

If you can get people wanting to work with you and wanting to join your project, then that offers a huge benefit straight from day one. You may not want all of them on your team, and you may want some people who haven't lined up begging to join the party, but at least you know that either you are popular to work with and/or the project you are heading up is seen as an exciting one with career potential for your would-be team members.

People will seek your project out for a number of reasons:

- You (your sheer charisma, track record of success, reputation for team support or development, etc.)
- Recommendation from others (based on the above list)
- The project (high profile, new and exciting, groundbreaking, business critical, etc.)
- The project opportunity (more senior project role, multi-company, multi-country, global, etc.)

All good things, I'm sure you would agree.

- Nothing better available

A bad thing without a doubt. Well possibly, but if this is a resource, you could really do with then it may work, or you just have to make it work.

Being popular is great, but be cautious and understand the motives that drive people towards you.

Get the best team that you can

A great old maxim for project teams is 'Something old, something new, something borrowed, something blue'[1]. Traditionally linked to the brides

DOI: 10.4324/9781003506522-52

outfit at weddings it can mean, for project, someone with experience (old), someone with enthusiasm (new), someone brought in to the team from outside the project/department etc who brings and objective viewpoint (borrowed), and someone not afraid to speak their minds and drive the team hard (blue – as in a little bit of swearing to make the point count).

Alternatively, you may be given a project team with little or no choice. At the very least try and get a known and skilled 'number two' to work with you, whether that is a support project manager, administrator, project office coordinator, whatever.

A 'good' project team is not just about the right skills but also about the right levels of enthusiasm and energy.

Feed the 'feelgood' factor

So once you have your team you need to help them bond quickly, work together productively (so you can be lazy and chill out in the comfy chair), and resolve problems in a calm way whilst communicating to each other, and you, in a simple effective manner. Simple really.

Your team, assuming that you have all your roles fulfilled, will need the following in order to be fully effective:

- Clarity of the goals of the project
- Belief in those goals
- Trust in you and their project colleagues
- Rules and processes for working
- Respect for each other

I would also add the ability and freedom to openly challenge anyone and anything, as long as that is done in a constructive and non-confrontational way.

With all this in place then the 'feelgood' factor can thrive, you just have to feed it now with your support and enthusiasm. (A reasonable budget for social activities doesn't do any harm either).

Consider is it nature or nurture?

It is a very lucky project manager that assumes control of a project and a project team and finds that they work at optimum performance from day one (all the way through to the day 'end'). No, the reality is that you will need to do some work to help make this happen.

Going back to the list above:

- Clarity of the goals of the project: this is your job to explain this clearly
- Belief in those goals: this is your job to ensure that you believe that they believe (if you don't even believe then there is no hope), and if they don't believe to convert them
- Trust in you and their project colleagues: this can only be achieved through experience, proving that trust is there day by day
- Rules and processes for working: again, this is up to you to present, educate, publish, promote and enforce
- Respect for each other: you must manage this; respect is an inherent human nature, but you do need to keep a close eye on this and deal with any instances where a lack of respect is identified
- Freedom to be open in their views: encourage this from day one, at project meetings, one-to-ones, team social events, audits and reviews and, at the end of projects, retrospectives. It is not just about being open to listening to people but also following up on suggestions and comments

Spot the carers

A lot of the above you need to do as the project manager, but mostly at the start of the project, Along the way you could identify project team members who are 'carers' or 'nurturers', and use them, it will help you, and it will make them feel good.

These people are closest to the Belbin[2] team role of 'Team worker', they are good listeners and diplomats, talented at smoothing over conflicts and helping parties understand each other without becoming confrontational. The beneficial effect of a 'Team worker' is often not noticed until they are absent, when the team begins to argue, and small but important things cease to happen.

These are the people who will naturally help others, quickly and without fuss, and will present issues to you that are not technical or operational but of a more personal nature.

Use all of your project team's skills and talents. Just because you recruited team member 'A' because of their known skill at technology 'X' does not mean that cannot unitise their personnel skill of 'Y' (where 'Y' could well be the skill of organising project social events, keeping tracking of team members birthdays, and being aware of any personal issues, etc.).

There is a lot of 'science' out there to help you analyse your project team members if you wish – already mentioned is Belbin, and there is also Myers-Briggs[3], for example. But equally you can learn a lot by just watching your team members working, in teams, alone, at meetings and so on. And in talking to them, don't forget that it is good to talk (and not just about project matters either).

Analyse the love required

As with communication, covered in an earlier chapter, you should 'customise' the love you give to the recipient. Everyone wants something different. Find out what they want and provide it – as long as it is earned.

Do it privately or publicly as is warranted, or indeed required by the recipient, and do try and avoid the 'Oscar speech[4]' syndrome where you thank everyone and their mother and their mother's pet poodle for this wonderful, wonderful project and all the wonderful support you have received and how you will miss them all so terribly. Keep it real!

Notes

1 The custom is based on an English poem: Something old, something new, something borrowed, something blue, and a silver sixpence in her shoe. The custom is that if the bride carries all four items on her wedding day, she will have a happy marriage. Each verse refers to a good luck item:

   • Something old: continuity with the bride's family and the past.
   • Something new: optimism and hope for the bride's new life ahead.
   • Something borrowed: an item from a happily married friend or family member, whose good fortune in marriage is supposed to carry over to the new bride.
   • Something blue: before the late 19th century, blue was a popular colour for wedding gowns.

2 The Belbin Team Role Inventory assesses how an individual behaves in a team environment. It is therefore a behavioural tool, subject to change, and not a psychometric instrument. The assessment includes 360-degree feedback from observers as well as the individual's own evaluation of their behaviour, and contrasts how they see their behaviour versus how their colleagues do. The Belbin Inventory scores people on how strongly they express traits from nine different Team Roles. An individual may and often does exhibit strong tendencies towards multiple roles.

3 The Myers-Briggs typology model regards personality type as similar to left- or right-handedness: individuals are either born with, or develop, certain preferred ways of thinking and acting. The MBTI sorts some of these psychological differences into four opposite pairs, or "dichotomies", with a resulting 16 possible psychological types. None of these types is "better" or "worse". The 16 different types are: Extraversion, Sensing, Thinking, Judging and then Introversion, Intuition, Feeling, Perceiving.

4 Greer Garson is credited with having given the longest acceptance speech in the history of the Academy Awards. The next year, speech length was capped. Legend tells of her oration being as long as 20 minutes, but in actual fact it was only about seven minutes (it just felt a lot longer).

A project manager's tale of inappropriate love

I was working on a project, not as the project manager this time, but in a quality support role that required my involvement in a part time manner over a period of months.

During that time, I was invited, as a matter of politeness I am sure, to a number of team social events.

The project had passed through a pilot phase and had been duly proven and ready for deployment at a number of locations across the UK, France and Germany. This roll out was managed by a team of people who had assisted in the pilot project and who had now graduated to ownership and management of the project proper.

As a risk precaution, my role was there to review key documents and milestones and generally make sure the project was in good health and on track.

Now this team liked to party. Well, they travelled around the countries, stayed in nice hotels, ate well on expenses (and it must be admitted, drank well on expenses too), as well as having a 'team building' budget that was quite impressive. The project manager was a gregarious guy who loved all things 'outdoors' and as a result the social events, that began with a few beers and a meal, progressed quickly through bowling and go-karting ever upwards until about 12 months in to the project, he came up with the biggie!

We were all on location number four that was in the process of going live and the project manager and most of the team were feeling very pleased with themselves. Time to party!

Now I had begun to notice that one member of the team, the guy who was in charge of preparing each location for deployment, was beginning to get a little less organised. The preparation work was being rushed it seemed and errors were being made that impacted the deployment work. The model was that he would spend a week on site ahead of the rest of the team to complete this preparation work, be joined by the full team whilst they deployed (this took four weeks in total) but leave them a week early in order to move on a prepare the next location.

DOI: 10.4324/9781003506522-53

Things came to a head during the time the full team was at the fourth location. First, the mistakes made in preparation this time caused a lot of problems and the team was less than happy about this. Fingers were angrily pointed at the 'Mr Preparation'. Second, the project manager decided to run a team building experience at the weekend – lots of fresh air, cold rivers, open fields, tall trees and bridge building with cocktail sticks and Coke cans (or something like that). I happened to be with the team at that point in time for one of my regular reviews.

Suddenly 'Mr P' went absent without leave – he just disappeared. It took two days to get confirmation that he had just checked out the hotel, jumped into his car and headed home.

Since I was only required on site for two days and had not been invited to the weekend experience of a lifetime, I volunteered to go and see 'Mr P' when I got back and see if I could find out what the problem was.

And so I did.

It turned out that out of all of the project team, our 'Mr P' was the only one married. The rest of the team were single or content not to spend so much time around their respective partners. In addition, 'Mr P' had no taste for the great outdoors or partying in general and actually preferred a much quieter life. And third, he felt that he had never received any praise for his work. He was alone on site doing the preparatory work, which had no glory attached to it; and he left site before the location went live and therefore missed the time when everyone was thanked for all their hard work.

'Mr P' was a good guy, a valuable asset to the team, good at his job. But, unconsidered and unknown by the rest of his team and his project manager, he had volunteered for this role for the very reason that he could avoid some of the partying and excesses of the rest of the team. He was so detached from the decision-making process that he had no say on the roll out schedule and as a result ended up with very little time to be at home. The rest of the team loved the fact that they were never at home and lived for 90 per cent of the time at the company's expense. And finally, his tastes were never considered when the social events were planned. To begin with, he joined in to be part of the team, but later on he joined in because he had to.

I can't say I was close enough or clever enough to have spotted this any earlier, but it was a good lesson I learned from the sideline. Consider what 'love' each of your team member's needs. In this case, even the most basic of information about one team member was not recognised by the rest.

Was there a happy ending? Well, initially he went back and trained another team member in his preparation duties with a plan to rotate the team roles a little, but this lasted less than six months. He eventually elected to take a job, within the same company, but close to home. Where he was happy.

The lights are on
(but no-one's at home)

Being accessible but in a controlled way

I'm all for being there for people, honest I am. It's just that people take advantage of it if I am.

So for the 'productive lazy' project manager, I would suggest that it is perfectly acceptable for the lights to be on and for no-one to be at home; not all of the time, obviously, and at critical times, access and visibility are all too important. But for the rest of the time, why not let the whole of the teamwork a few things out for themselves, take some degree of responsibility and decision-making and generally get on with the tasks at hand.

Being there when you are really needed and being there all the time are very different things indeed.

Being reachable in a controlled manner, and within an acceptable timeframe, to answer appropriate questions (and not stupid ones) is equally important. The last thing you want is a long line of people queuing up at your desk waiting to ask advice and you phone flashing with an ever-increasing number of messages, all the time while your inbox is reaching capacity with incoming demands for your attention.

This can lead to the 'lights on all the time' syndrome, a very dangerous condition:

"What should I do now?"

"Breathe", you might reply.

"In or out?"

You have so many other more useful things that you could be doing, like reading a good book in the comfy chair, for example.

DOI: 10.4324/9781003506522-54

Applying the 'Productive Lazy' approach

Avoid the swamp

This is linked in so many ways to the communication topic already covered. If you create a communication plan that guarantees to swamp you from day one, what is the benefit; to you or to the project? None.

The plan should ensure you are not seen as the oracle for all matters, nor that you are the bottleneck for a constructive information flow within the project team. Most projects develop communication plans in a certain way; that is as a plan that is the documented strategy for getting the right information to the right people at the right time. We all know that each stakeholder has different requirements for information and so the plan defines what, how and how often communications should be made. What project managers rarely do is consider and map all communication flows, official, unofficial, developmental, or complete, and do a load analysis across the project structure of these communication flows. If they did, they would spot bottlenecks much earlier on that they normally do, usually this is only identified when one part of the communication chain starts complaining about their workload.

Consider the open door policy

The 'open door' policy has become a real management cliché.

"Of course", managers pronounce in a firm voice, "my door is always open to you all, day, or night; I'm really there for you".

Empowerment in this way has become more an entitlement for the project team than a project manager's choice; they just expect you to be there when they want you to be (and not even when they need you to be there either). An 'open door' policy can easily transform a project manager's role from that of an authority, and managing, figure, to that of a subservient accommodator with little chance for exercising control on those that demand access to them.

DOI: 10.4324/9781003506522-55

Be a good manager

The best manager is probably the one who reads the paper or MSN every morning, has time enough to say 'hi' at the coffee machine or isn't always running flat out because they are 'late for an important meeting'. By that I mean that a good (an obviously 'productively lazy') manager has everything running smoothly enough that they have time to read the paper or MSN and so on. This is a manager who has to be confident in their position and capabilities.

A good manager will have time for their project team, and, being one who has everything running smoothly, will allow that to happen.

A good manager does not to be on hand 24 hours a day, seven days a week. They do not have to have the answer to every question, nor do they have to be the conduit to the answer to every question. There is a whole project team out there – go talk to some of them – they will probably have a much better answer to hand anyway.

Think about number one

You honestly want the best for yourself as well as for the project; I understand that, so give yourself that chance. Have you ever met a project manager who has put themselves down as a project risk? "Yeah, well I am just too nice a guy, can't say no, can't turn someone away, love to chat" – likelihood 80 per cent, impact 100 per cent, mitigate now!

But hopefully by now you also want to apply the productive lazy approach, so consider this: let the team deal with 80 per cent of the communication, 80 per cent of the questions, 80 per cent of the issues and let the 20 Per cent come through you for consideration and guidance. You don't even have to 'solve' that 20 per cent. I would further suggest that only 20 per cent of this 20 per cent are likely to be answered by yourself in an adequate manner; there are always others that can better advice.

Think about the rest

OK, you have dealt with the 'thinking about number one' thing, now what about your team? Well, by dealing with 'number one', you will have already done the team a huge favour. You will be accessible when you need to be accessible. The lights will go on as and when they are really needed – it is a kind of 'green' project management policy.

The worst thing that can happen is that just at the moment when there is a 'clear and present' need for someone to speak to you, whether that be on a project or on a personal matter, you are just too tied up with a whole pile of nothing to even give them the time of day. Remember the whole 'respect' and 'reputation for team support' team thing we spoke about earlier, well this is a major contributor the that.

Analyse and reduce

And this is not a one-off action; you need to keep on top of this as well. Projects change, communications develop, and roles flux. Do a quick analysis of what information and queries flow through you, and how, and regularly re-assess. Can others deal with some of this? What are the important components that you should be involved in? Are there too many questions and communication from certain sources? And so on.

Make sure that everyone knows that the lights will go on and when and how they can turn that light on fast, if they really need to.

A project manager's tale about the importance of position

This one is not my tale; it is the story of a friend of mine, a friend who is, of course, a project manager. A project manager who I know to be very good at team building, a real 'people' person.

Picture a new project with a new project office. Apparently, the company my friend was working for had reserved some brand-new office space in a building that they were going to move other departments in to in the coming months. In the meantime, the project team could take over one floor.

Now, I have been in many project offices over the years ranging from a single desk to a temporary office unit (grey boxes that get lifted into place by a crane and officially described as 'relocatable and modular accommodation' apparently). But by all accounts, this new building that my friend moved in to with his project team was superb.

He chose a nice new desk by a window and with a view facing the doors, so that he could see all that went on, people coming and going, working (or not working I guess) and so on.

And so life was good, and thus did the project move forwards in a pleasing way.

The only feature that was lacking was a decent coffee machine. They had a just a kettle to begin with, but the team waited with bated breath for the new, top of the range, super-dooper, hot beverage dispenser.

And we all know that the coffee machine is on the critical path to project success!

It arrived one weekday morning, wheeled in on a trolley barrow. My friend was elsewhere at the time on important project business. When he arrived back in the project office, he was somewhat surprised to see that his desk now had a new neighbour. A coffee machine.

"Hey, grab a coffee. It's great!", was the general cry from the project team. I am sure that that is what he did, before walking the two feet back to his desk.

DOI: 10.4324/9781003506522-56

The project office was full now, and so it was too late to move desk. Oh well, a great project office with a great coffee machine was not something to make too much fuss about.

And then things went downhill:

Day 1: People started saying 'hello' each time they lined up for a coffee at the machine by his desk.

Day 2: People started conversations as they waited for their freshly simulated brewed cup of java by his desk.

Day 3: People started sitting on his desk, while they waited for coffee, said 'hello', engaged in conversation and were generally sociable.

Day 4: People asked him where the spare coffee cups were and what 'error 54g' was.

Day 5: People asked him what the telephone number for the coffee repairman was so that they could report 'error 54g' and get the coffee machine fixed.

Day 10: People started using the phone on his desk while waiting for a coffee, etc.

Day 15: The project manager left the building.

In actual fact he did move desks: he manage to secure a small space across the landing from the main project office. It wasn't idealm as he was now removed from the project team, but, on balance, it was better than the alternative.

It doesn't matter that you want to run an 'open door' policy in order to be as accessible to everyone, if you want to get on with your job you do need some 'space'. To be right at the centre of everything all of the time is not conducive to being a good project manager.

It was the coffee machine or the project manager, and the team made it clear that the coffee machine won, hands down!

Chapter 8

Productivity – Change

Continuing the personal productivity road, we underscore the significance of honesty and positivity in managing workload and fostering personal growth. It advocates for a balanced approach to task management, emphasising the need to reduce your own Work in Progress limit to enhance flexibility and prevent burnout. By honestly assessing time commitments and prioritising tasks strategically, individuals can ensure they leave room for unforeseen opportunities while maintaining productivity.

Exploring then the impact of influence and relationships on personal development. It highlights the importance of surrounding yourself with supportive individuals who encourage positive change and offers practical advice for evaluating and cultivating beneficial connections. Ultimately, providing insights into overcoming challenges such as procrastination and emphasises the value of staying motivated and focused on the path to success.

DOI: 10.4324/9781003506522-57

Be honest and be positive

Think about this: every time you reduce your 'work in progress' (WIP) limit, the amount or percentage of your time that is committed at any given moment to tasks and jobs underway, then you are automatically improving your flexibility for addressing new activities without impacting on this WIP. You are effectively increasing your 'not work in progress' (NWIP), the amount or percentage of your time that is not committed at any given moment.

If you don't take this approach and you 'run to the max' all of the time, you will naturally:

- Burn yourself out at some point
- Hit times when you have more to do than you can physically (and mentally) handle

Many of us can be hugely effective when under extreme pressure, and that is great, but it is not a sustainable model – something will give eventually, and it is most likely to be you.

Flexible working is a key way of achieving real success, in not disappointing anyone you have commitments with, but in being open and ready as and when new 'work' appears on the immediate horizon.

For all you know, in the next 24 hours that 'opportunity' that you had longed for might just turn up in the post, through a meeting, as part of a phone call, and how will you feel if you have to decline the chance to get on board, join in or take ownership all because you were just too committed already?

Or perhaps something that you didn't anticipate happens that demands your immediate attention and, as a result, you have to drop something else that you really wanted (and needed) to do?

In both cases you will be disappointed, but it will be because you planned it this way. You didn't allow yourself the flexibility to be versatile – 100 per cent is not a good thing.

DOI: 10.4324/9781003506522-58

Try this quick exercise to check your 'versatility' factor:

1. Think about your next working day – how many hours in the day will you be active, that is not sleeping? This is your finite capacity (unless you are capable of time travel) for 'doing stuff'.
2. OK, now list all of the things that you have to do. Include everything: eating, washing, travelling, emails, meetings, phone calls, personal activities, social communication, etc.
3. Now allocate time in hours or parts of hours against each task – it is important here that you be very, very honest with yourself. Don't kid yourself that you only spend ten minutes emailing each day, or that you can get to the office in under 25 minutes.
4. Right, now you can add it all up... actually before you do that just go back over the estimates of time once more for me and give yourself a last chance to be really, truly, completely and utterly honest with yourself. Change the numbers if your conscience tells you to do so and then add it all up again...

Don't miss out on opportunities because you were too busy!

So what did you end up with? How many hours out of your finite capacity limit have you committed?

What percentage is left free to deal with the unplanned and unexpected?

If it is less than 20 per cent[1], then I feel that you are kidding yourself a little and would recommend that you look again at what is on that list and what you could perhaps not do, do less of, get help with and so on.

We saw earlier about a journey. 'It is a little like going for a walk, there are two types of walks: the 'A' to 'B' type where the purpose is to get to 'B' from a starting point of 'A'. And there is the second type where you have plenty of time and the pleasure in the walk is to take your time and discover interesting places on the way. For a 'productive but lazy' person the 'A' to 'B' journey is the one to go for – in fact in a truly 'productively lazy' approach you would see if you could in fact miss out 'B' altogether and go straight to 'C', if 'C' was your next destination. Well, by allowing yourself the right degree of flexibility, occasionally, you can opt to take the slower, more scenic journey and find some new and interesting sights.

Take the time now to consider the list that you have made and, as a start, aim to reduce or eliminate at least one of the items on that list – and hey, that shouldn't be 'eating' or 'breathing'!

Remember:

Think – Plan – Prioritise – Focus

There is a glass of water on the table...

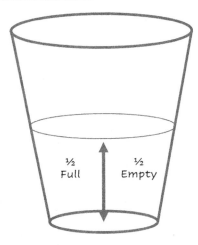

Figure 8.1.1 Half full or half empty.

One man might say, 'It's half-full.' He is traditionally considered an optimist.

A second man might say, 'It's half-empty.' He is traditionally considered a pessimist.

A third man might say 'It's twice as big as it needs to be.' He is probably a management consultant and will give you a bill to back up his analysis.

But the productively lazy person should say: 'The glass is fine, and the drink is fine, it is just right to be topped up, should I become thirsty or if someone offers to buy me another drink or quickly emptied, should some free champagne suddenly appear.

Note

1 Hey, look at that, we are back with the good old 80/20 rule once more. Incidentally, the Pareto Principle was a prominent part of the 2007 bestseller *The 4-Hour Work Week* by Tim Ferriss, in which the author recommended focusing one's attention on that 20 per cent that contributes 80 per cent of your income. More notably, he also recommends firing those 20 per cent of customers who take up the majority of one's time and cause the most trouble. In terms of your personal priorities, you might want to think about 'firing' the 20 per cent of activities that are least important, so that you can do a better job on the 80 per cent that do matter and be flexible for new opportunities.

Are we there yet?

As a small child, I could never understand why we seemed to drive for so long in the family car to get somewhere special for a day out. As the minutes and sometimes hours were consumed in travel I would look out of my window and see interesting place after interesting place go by. What was wrong with stopping at that park?

That wood? That river? Why did we have to keep going to the specific destination of parental choice?

In the end, we always arrived somewhere good and had a great day out, but I would have been just as happy (or so I thought) stopping earlier and enduring less 'car time'.

My perceived 'point of success' as far as a day out was concerned was a whole lot earlier than my parents. Who knows, maybe I've always been lazy (in a good way, of course).

But we have now reached the last two of the five key questions set at the beginning of this book:

- If you have to do it, then what is the shortest path to the point of success?
- What exactly is that point of success, and at what stage will you just be wasting your time?

If you have to do it and you want to do it, then what is it that you actually have to do? What is the shortest path to the point of success? We are all driven by the desire to do a great job if at all possible, but there is a difference between delivering to the task and delivering beyond the task. Performance over and beyond the call of duty can be appropriate in some cases, particularly if you are dealing with someone for the first time perhaps and trying to win them over in some way, but in most cases, it isn't appropriate or beneficial to anyone.

How do you go about identifying exactly that point of success beyond which you will just be wasting your time?

DOI: 10.4324/9781003506522-59

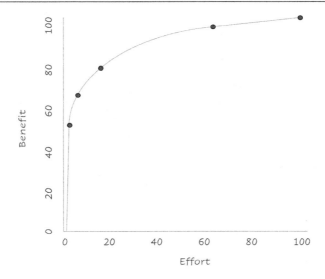

Figure 8.2.1 The sweet spot of effort.

What you need to do is identify the 'sweet spot', which can be defined as the point where the cumulative return of your personal effort outweighs the benefit of the enhanced deliverable. There is an average guide to aid you here – the good old 80/20 rule is back in action and showing the way.

Yes, 20 per cent of the effort delivers 80 per cent of the benefit.

Easy! Well maybe so, but do your homework here and make sure that in each situation or case, the 80 per cent benefit is safe and suitable.

All you have to do is decide if that 80 per cent benefit is enough for the purposes of this specific task or not, and if not, what percentage will be. What will drive this decision will include:

• Quality standards, safety standards, legal requirements, or other rigid governance protocols.

Assuming that we are not talking about such matters, this decision will be driven by:

• Personal satisfaction. What level will you put on the satisfaction limit – the danger here is to over-deliver, just because you enjoy doing the activity, which is all well and good if you have the time available, but not productive if you don't.
• Desire to please. How much are you trying to satisfy others? This may be a regular job that can be done to an acceptable level, and people will be happy, or this may be a situation when you really want to impress.

Try to find the 'sweet spot' every time you engage in an activity; it should be part of the planning stage of everything you do.

Don't over-engineer it – don't over-resource it – don't overcomplicate it – and don't overdo what only needs to be done, to the level of 'just enough'. But don't cut corners either.

Repetition of tasks, completing recovery work, duplication of effort – all waste time and are counterproductive – so why take that path when you are striving to be efficient in everything else you do? There is little value in working towards a focused and simple 'to do' list only to increase the required effort of each task through sloppy low-quality work which will push you back up to your maximum capacity once again. Pointless!

Influence and relationships

In order to be different in some way and change from what you are, or were if you have started already, then you will definitely need some help (beyond a good book and guide like this one) along the way.

Here are two ways to understand what and who around you offer influence, good or not so good, and how to adjust your current network of influence to help you achieve what you wish to achieve.

When I reflect back, I can see that many people have influenced me over the years but mostly I didn't realise it at the time.

"You don't have to be a "person of influence" to be influential. In fact, the most influential people in my life are probably not even aware of the things they've taught me".

Scott Adams

Let's start off with the influence of five.

It is said that we are the average of the five people we most closely associate with[1]. So, if you are one of those five people closest to others then you have a great opportunity to promote yourself, your personal desires, and your work. If you present enthusiasm at all (reasonable) times, then you really can influence others around you.

It is also said that enthusiasm is contagious (but so is the lack of it) so be careful and be positive. At all times, even the difficult times, present what you are trying to achieve in a way that is:

- Positive: as we have seen your enthusiasm can be infectious and engaging with people about the positive aspects of what you, and they, are doing can only be a good thing.
- Good for everyone involved: listen to people's views and try to identify the challenges that others face that you may be able to address or help with.

DOI: 10.4324/9781003506522-60

- The right thing to do: talk about the 'greater good' for everyone involved or associated with the change.

Of course you need to keep an open mind and be seen as someone who does consider the views of others.

Consider yourself as the extra one to the five as well. By that I mean it is not just a matter of you being freely influenced by others around you, there is a strong connection to your spirit, personality, and strength of character as to how much you are influenced, and indeed how much you influence others.

Now you might consider, as you want to change in some positive way, assessing your own 'relationship of five'. Who are they? Are these the best influencers to aid your journey? Who could you connect with in order to help you further?

Try this assessment right now:

Question: Who are the five people you spend the most time within your life right now[2]?

- What are they like?
- What are their top three qualities?
- What proportion of your time do you spend with them?

OK good, now try this:

Question: What is it that you would like to change?

- What is the ideal that you wish to become?
- What are the qualities you want to possess?
- Where will your journey take you?

And finally:

- Do the five people you are now connected to match most closely who you want to become in the future? To be clear, I am not suggesting dumping those around you and going cold-heartedly out to find five new (better) relationships – absolutely not. I am just suggesting that change is easier when you are well supported in this process. If you are constantly surrounded by negative, fear-based people in your life, it will have an impact on who you eventually become and your progression in life.

Here's another question, well a question in two parts actually.

1. Question: Among those people that you know, who is the number one person you would aspire to be like, who embodies what it is that you would like to change?

2. Question: Among those people that you know of who is the number one person you would aspire to be like, who embodies what it is that you would like to change? The difference with this question is that you can pick anybody at all – even though you might not know them. They may or may not be famous. They may or may not be alive. They may be anyone, anywhere.

Now for the first person consider how you would get closer to them, to be influenced more by them, make them become one of your five influencers.

And for the person that you only know of, but do not have contact with, how can you get closer to them in some way?

Well, you could try contacting them; you never know what might happen. Most people now have in place some means of communicating with them (or their representatives) through email, social networks, websites, letters, phone calls and so on.

If direct contact doesn't work out for you then you can always effectively engage with the essence of that person in the form of their works: books, blogs, articles, webcasts, training courses or materials, presentations that you could attend or listen to recordings of, television shows or radio shows, or any other way that you can make an indirect connection.

And now we look at the relationship of six.

A 'degree of separation' is a measure of social distance between people[3]. You are one degree away from everyone you know, two degrees away from everyone they know, and so on. Think of it as a vast spider web connecting you in some way to everyone else.

A personal network then is a set of human contacts known to an individual, with whom that individual would expect to interact at intervals to support a given set of activities. That status of 'knowing' does not necessarily mean that there is deep knowledge or understanding between the parties involved, rather that they are connected in some way and have some form of mutual interest or background.

Personal networks are intended to be mutually beneficial – extending the concept of teamwork beyond the immediate peer group. The term is often encountered in the workplace, though these days it could apply equally to other pursuits outside work.

Such networking is usually undertaken over an extended period and, these days, there are many technology-based means to aid such networking – connecting, tracking, updating, sharing and communicating – and to scale networks in a global fashion[4].

It could be through such a network that you could in fact reach out and connect to that person that you would like to have as one of your influencers but that you only know of[5].

One of the great lessons I have learned as I have personally explored building my networks is that, for the greater part, people are happy and willing to help out. Of course, you have to be ready to reciprocate, that is how it all works. I have been surprised many times over at how quickly I can contact someone I wanted to reach – other authors and speakers, many of whom I had been fans of for some time – and at how willing they all were to communicate with me and aid me.

Start thinking about who you would like to connect with, why this is so, and how they might help you (and be ready to offer your help in return). Who do you now know who might start you on the path to connection with your end target?

By considering who is now influencing you and who would better influence you, you can, in some way, bring about a change through other people.

The journey is always easier with others by your side and ready to give you a positive comment or a guiding suggestion.

Notes

1 'You are the average of the five people you spend the most time with,' suggested Jim Rohn, motivational speaker and self-help guru. Jim Rohn (1930–2009) was an American entrepreneur, author and motivational speaker. His rags to riches story played a large part in his work, which influenced others in the personal development industry.

2 I would focus on adults here although it is surprising how influential your children can be.

3 Six degrees of separation (also referred to as the 'human spider web') refers to the idea that everyone is, on average, approximately six steps away from any other person on Earth, so that a chain of, 'a friend of a friend' statements can be made, on average, to connect any two people in six steps or fewer. It was originally set out by Frigyes Karinthy and popularised in a play written by John Guare.

4 I am not going to list them here, you all know what they are, but I am on most of them so feel free to connect. I am not promising to be a good influencer for you, but I am happy to share my network to our mutual advantage if possible.

5 The game 'Six Degrees of Kevin Bacon' was invented as a play on the concept. The goal is to link any actor to Kevin Bacon through no more than six connections, where two actors are connected if they have appeared in a movie or commercial together.

When the going gets tough*

The path to productive laziness will not necessarily be a smooth one.

It is possible that despite all of this thinking and planning and focusing, the clear plan of action, the short and pertinent 'to do' list you might hit the wall of inaction, the quicksand of apathy, the jungle of procrastination. And you stop.

If this happens here are two tips that may get you moving:

1. Read Eat that Frog! by Brian Tracy[1] (easy, insightful and useful).
2. Go and do something completely different. Go with what really gets you going, what truly excites you. If you are uninspired to do something, then it is probably because that something seems very boring to you. If so, move on to something that doesn't seem so boring, something far more exciting. Come up with a list of things you could do that are important and productive and still exciting and go with those tasks. You will be avoiding something boring for sure, but you will be motivated to do the other, more exciting stuff. And when you have regained your energy and enthusiasm you will often find that you tackle the boring stuff with enthusiasm and success – you just needed to get motivated.

Interestingly I have found, many times over, that even when you hit that 'wall' and go off and do something more exciting, the something else that you have done turns out to be useful pretty soon afterwards. I am not sure if this is because you tend to do things that you know in the back of your mind might be useful or relevant, or you think in terms of 'how can I reuse that great stuff I put together a while ago' when problem solving, or maybe a combination of both.

* 'When the going gets tough, the tough get going' is a popular saying. The phrase has been attributed both to Joseph P. Kennedy, father of the US President John F. Kennedy, and to Norwegian-born American football player and coach, Knute Rockne. A song of the same name was recorded by Billy Ocean in 1985.

DOI: 10.4324/9781003506522-61

Either way it does seem that very little of what I do, even in these moments of re-motivation, ends up being wasted.

Go with the pulse!

The question of single or multi-tasking might also arise. In reality, we can't survive without multi-tasking (even the men). I mean, if all we could cope with was 'breathe in, breathe out' then that would pretty much wipe out the whole self-help book genre, among a lot of other things.

But which approach delivers the best progress?

We thought earlier about the whole 'more haste, less speed' principle that makes us, when we are in a hurry, more often end up completing the task in a slower time, due to making mistakes on the way and having to rework stuff or put in recovery effort.

We also covered the fact that, typically, only 20 per cent of what you do really matters because it is that effort that delivers 80 per cent of the results required. Linked to that you should therefore allow yourself to concentrate and focus on the really important stuff at times. So I would suggest that it is perfectly acceptable in these situations to single task; not all of the time obviously, but when something is that important, then you don't want any distractions.

The rest of the time it is definitely multi-tasking all the way. But consider this: although multi-tasking does have its benefits, there are times when it can get a bit overwhelming. Taking on a lot of work you tend to spread yourself too thinly and the law of diminishing returns begins to take effect.

I find that my efficiency rises with the more work I do, within reason, and drops as tasks get longer and more detailed. Therefore I approach work in a series of 'pulses' doing a little here and a little there that all add up to a final result or delivery. Taking this approach keeps me fresh and alert, interested and focused, and allows me to effectively 'prototype' small packets of effort to identify the best outcome or solution. When something doesn't work then I haven't wasted whole heaps of time, and I can easily redirect my efforts and stay positive.

Note

1 In his book *Eat That Frog!*, author Brian Tracy helps you to stop procrastinating and be more effective in managing your time. The key to reaching high levels of performance and productivity is to develop the lifelong habit of tackling your major task first thing each morning. There's an old saying that if you eat a live frog in the morning, nothing worse can happen for the rest of the day. Your 'frog' should be the most difficult item on your to-do list.

Chapter 9

Laziness – Then Thick Again at the Far End

Finally, in the final stages of a project, we acknowledge that amidst the temptation to celebrate and move on to the next endeavour, there lies a crucial opportunity for growth and learning. Conducting a lesson learned process and retrospective allows project managers to uncover known unknowns and even unknown unknowns, tapping into the collective wisdom of the team and filling in knowledge gaps. By embracing this 'productive laziness', teams can ensure future projects are even more successful with less effort, leading to more time for relaxation and strategic planning.

This approach underscores the importance of finishing what was started and actively seeking to understand both known and unknown aspects of the project. Through open dialogue and structured retrospectives, teams can unearth valuable lessons and move along the path of self-development from unconscious incompetence to unconscious competence.

Yet, despite these clear benefits, the question remains: why do some project managers fail to learn from past experiences, perpetuating a cycle of repetition? It's a question that prompts reflection on the essence of project management and the need for continuous improvement to break free from the cycle of 'insanity'.

DOI: 10.4324/9781003506522-62

Time for one last effort

Just to make life easier in the future.

The Lazy Project Manager's Theory of Projects, from a Productive Laziness aspect:

> *"All projects are thick at one end, much, much thinner in the middle and then thick again at the far end".*

Now is not the time to declare the project a success and rush off for a Bloody Mary[1] at the bar.

No, now is the time that you can apply a small and final amount of effort but gain enormous amounts of knowledge so that future projects are likely to be even more successful and potentially with even less effort. And by less effort we know that means so much more time in the 'comfy chair' being lazy but in a productive way.

> *"The world is round and the place which may seem like the end may also be only the beginning".*

> Ivy Baker Priest[2]

Notes

1 I am not advocating that project managers need to drink alcohol. An alternative recipe to a Bloody Mary (my favourite cocktail) is a Virgin Mary: 4 ounces Tomato Juice, one teaspoon Worcestershire Sauce, one dash Lemon Juice, two drops Tabasco Sauce, Pepper and Salt. Stir with ice in a large wine glass. Garnish with a wedge of lime. Very nice – as is the 'GPMO' cocktail that I have developed for my own PMO – hey, you have to have your own customised cocktail in life.

2 Ivy Baker Priest was an American politician who served as Treasurer of the United States from 1953 to 1961 and California State Treasurer from 1967 to 1975.

DOI: 10.4324/9781003506522-63

The Missing Link

Either you have been missing something, or nothing has really been going on:

"As we know, there are known knowns
There are things we know we know
We also know there are known unknowns
That is to say, we know there are some things we do not know
But there are also unknown unknowns
The ones we don't know we don't know".

Donald Rumsfeld[1]

That is one crazy set of words, but actually there is a lot of sense in the whole thing.

Here you are at the end of the project. It has been a success, or, at the very least, is has not been a complete failure, and you are about to head off to the next project. But wait. Do you really honestly know everything? Do you know what you don't know? Well of course you don't; you can't possibly. So don't fool yourself that you do!

So what do you do about it? Well, what you do about it is to do something about it – now is the time to conduct a retrospective of your project, a review, a considered and open activity that will allow you the opportunity to learn what it is you don't yet know.

Just as at the start of the project, remember 'a brand shiny new project… at a point in time that is full of peace and love and general wellbeing between all parties involved', well the end of the project is a special time as well. It is a time when project team members are far more likely to talk to you openly, equally and honestly. Therefore it is a time you should really focus some effort on to learn how to be more effective (and even more 'Productively Lazy') next time around.

DOI: 10.4324/9781003506522-64

Note

1 12 February 2002, Department of Defense news briefing. Donald Henry Rumsfeld was an American politician, government official and businessman who served as Secretary of Defense from 1975 to 1977 under President Gerald Ford and again from 2001 to 2006 under President George W. Bush. He was both the youngest and the oldest secretary of defense in American history.

Applying the 'Productive Lazy' approach

Finish what you started

As the Mastermind[1] question master says, "I've started, and so I will finish", and you should make sure that you do the same. Finish the project in a correct and complete manner. Avoid all of those normal pressures and temptations to head off on the next juicy project that is calling you to.

Make the very most of this second opportunity of peace, love and harmony (hopefully) and learn everything that you can learn. It will be worth it, I guarantee.

Know what you know

Start first with yourself. What do you 'know' about the project? Well, a whole bunch of stuff, that's for sure, but what focus less on what you already knew at the start of the project and think more about what you have learnt new during the project.

Much of what happened will have been processed, dealt with, handled through the reapplication of past experience or knowledge, but some will have not. You learn through each project, so consider what it is that you learnt this time.

Now you know what you know and probably also know what you don't know, gaps in your experience on the project, questions you can ask your team.

Find out what you don't know

Now focus on the unknown unknowns.

The ideal way to do this is to conduct a full retrospective. If you can't do this, then at least gather input from key members of your project team. One the best reference books for this is *Project Retrospectives* by Norman L. Kerth. I love the prime directive that Kerth governs his retrospectives by; Regardless of what we discover, we must understand and truly believe that

DOI: 10.4324/9781003506522-65

everyone did the best job he or she could, given what was known at the time, his or her skills and abilities, the resources available and the situation at hand.

There are treasures out there. No single person knows all there is to know about the project, and certainly not you, the project manager (you don't honestly think your team told everything that went on, do you?).

So go gold mining. There are nuggets of gold in 'lessons learned' or at least lessons to be learned if only we pay attention. At least one of your project team will tell you something that will aid you in the future and let you be a little more productively lazy. And the best way to make this happen is to plan for it to happen, right back at the 'thick' front-end of the project, back at the very beginning.

Ask what you now need to know

As part of this retrospective process, make sure that you also take the opportunity to ask questions that you want answering. Remember? The things that you know you don't know, the gaps in your experience on the project, the questions that you should ask your team.

Complete your knowledge by having an open and honest dialogue with the team. It may surprise them what you don't know, and they will no doubt be pleased that they were able to help out during the project.

Learn the lessons to be learned

OK, now let's sum all this up. Carefully and slowly.

- You know what you know.
- You also know what you don't know – and received answers on the gaps in your knowledge hopefully.
- You now know what you didn't know you knew, through feedback from the team and other sources.
- And, through the retrospective, you at least know a little more about what you didn't know that you didn't know – if the team have been very open with you.

Simple, isn't it?

Tell others what you now know

And finally, don't just sit on that knowledge. Share it out among everyone that could benefit from it.

Lessons learned should be lessons shared, so don't be mean. Share it out!

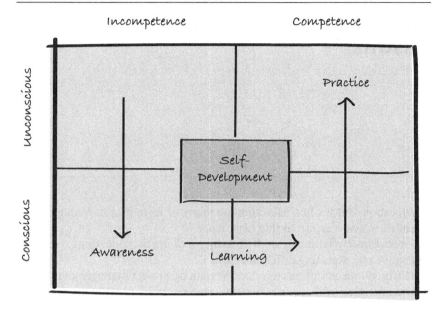

Figure 9.3.1 Competence model.

Time for one last grid[2]: the grid of self-development logic.

All the above can be summarised in this diagram. To move from unconscious incompetence to conscious incompetence, not knowing what you don't know and just not caring, you need awareness – the retrospective can aid this awareness.

To move from conscious incompetence to conscious competence, knowing what you don't know but caring about that fact – again the retrospective can aid, along with a learning plan based on the outputs.

And finally, to move from conscious competence to unconscious competence. Well, this just requires a lot of practice, so get to it!

Notes

1 Mastermind is a British quiz show, well known for its challenging questions, intimidating setting and air of seriousness. The basic format of Mastermind has never changed: four contestants face two rounds, one on a specialised subject of the contestant's choice; the other a general knowledge round.

2 I am sure that you have noticed my affection for all things 'grid'-like. We all know that a picture is supposed to paint a thousand words, or something like that, and a picture is easier to remember. Therefore, logically, a simple picture is that much easier to remember, when you need to.

Why don't we learn these lessons?

The question that is often asked among many of us in project management is 'why didn't we learn from that experience?'

Albert Einstein famously said: "Insanity is doing the same thing over and over again and expecting different results".

So why do we accept 'insanity' as the path of project management?

The next time you are in a meeting, just try this out. Whether you are presenting or someone else it doesn't matter but what happens when the inevitable happens, you go to write something on the flipchart, or the whiteboard and the pen is dry. How many of you (and I freely admit I am just as guilty) put the pen down on the rack again, pick up another one and carry on with the key, interesting, important point you were making. Thereby leaving the same dry pen for the next person – or worse, for yourself to do the same thing again a little later in the meeting.

Did you expect the pen to magically refill itself? Of course not. Madness!

Did you put the pen in the bin and ensure that a new one was put in its place, or at least noted for someone that new pens were required? Of course not. Madness!

A simple lesson in lessons learned, or the process of not learning to be more precise.

So, are we programmed to not learn lessons?

Clearly not. If that was the case, then we would have wiped ourselves out as a race a long, long, long time ago.

So why don't we learn lessons when it comes to project experiences?

Well, I think that in actual fact we do, or personally we do. Our personal project experience has to be a learning experience (even if that learning experience is 'I am getting out of project management and finding a real job to do…').

No, we do learn, and we do progress and grow as project managers, and we are all the better for it.

DOI: 10.4324/9781003506522-66

The challenge comes from sharing the knowledge of those lessons among others and in learning from others' experience in return. It is a matter of scale and capability all mixed in with time and priorities.

It is not the process of binning the empty pen and replacing the pen but in letting others know what and why you did that and how it can benefit them in the future and why they should also pass on this piece of knowledge.

It is less 'lessons learned' than 'lessons shared'.

OK, the next time you go to write something on the flipchart, or the whiteboard and the pen is dry stop – turn to face your audience and say "Right, this pen is going in the bin, and let me tell you why …".

Learning

The first part is relatively easy – you either provide a mechanism for team members to record their personal lessons learnt during the project or, preferably, organise individual or team meetings to exchange ideas and thoughts, advice and experience.

There is an immediate challenge here in that project team resources have often already moved on to another project and capturing lessons learned is never seen as a priority. But to improve future project delivery efficiency, and to adopt best practices, it is essential to capture such lessons.

So let's assume that you crack this first challenge:

* Your organisation buys in big time to the value of lessons learned
* You allow team members the time to discuss and record lessons learned at the end of a project

But there is more; you don't just sit on that knowledge you have to share it out among everyone that could benefit from it. Lessons learned should be lessons shared.

But here we encounter an even bigger challenge – how?

Sharing

Yes, here there lies a problem – often a big fat hairy problem with pointy teeth and a really bad attitude.

How do you effectively share lessons?

Right, I guess we have to start with the 'science bit', but it is important to understand how wisdom comes about and also why knowledge is so hard to share effectively sometimes.

The DIKW Pyramid, also known variously as the 'DIKW Hierarchy' or 'Wisdom Hierarchy', refers loosely to one of a series of models for representing purported structural and/or functional relationships between data, information, knowledge and wisdom.

- Typically, information is defined in terms of data
- Knowledge in terms of information
- And wisdom in terms of knowledge

In 1987 Czechoslovakian-born educator Milan Zeleny[1] mapped the elements of the hierarchy to these knowledge forms:

- Know-nothing
- Know-what
- Know-how
- And know-why

The 'DIKW' model proposes that data by itself has no meaning; it just fills databases and could, for example, be all of the hours of effort recorded against a project, a big number probably but in itself meaningless.

Information arises when humans examine this data and provide a framework for understanding what the data represents. In this project I can see that 'x' hours were spent on this project task and 'y' on this task when both were expected to take 'z' hours.

Knowledge is the ability to take an action, and it is created when information is used by individuals and organisations to devise a course of action and, often, this course of action is to generate more data thereby resulting in a new Data–Information–Knowledge cycle. In this project, by assessing all of the time effort recorded, we can see that there are variances that negatively impacted the schedule, if we compare this to another project using the same resources, we can identify like variances with some of those resources.

Wisdom encompasses the best and most appropriate action, and it usually results from multiple rounds of the Data-Information-Knowledge cycle. In our future projects we have learnt that if we use resource 'A', we would need to factor the effort estimates by '1.2' and for resource 'B' by '1.3' in order to achieve the expected schedule results.

It has to be said that the 'DIKW' model has its non-fans shall we say but it still allows us to think through the process of embedded lessons learned from our projects.

We have a lot – an awful lot – of data at the end of projects, and we also have the overall 'gut' feeling of how it went and where the problems were. We can validate these 'gut' experiential feelings with information if so required and this will allow us to create or test knowledge and then move on to record wisdom.

But then we hit the 'how' issue.

We also hit the 'really' question.

The 'how' is all about the mechanism for sharing. Say you finish a project and you list five lessons learned that you feel are 'wisdom' that needs to be shared. You are one of 200 projects on the company portfolio, and each year another 100 projects are kicked off, and you have 1,000 people around the world in 25 countries that need to know … everything ideally. That is a heap of wisdom exchange, added to which every one of those 1,000 people are really busy[2].

Oh, and they speak 15 different native languages[3].

Oh, and they don't have time to search for information in some vast difficult to access and hard to sort database[4].

And the 'really' question – well, is this really in any way 'best practice' or even 'good practice', or was it just 'practice that somehow manage to get us out of the 'doodoo' on this particular project and really shouldn't be used again if at all possible, to avoid it?

The problem that arises here is that in order to sift out real 'wisdom', that is reusable, you need 'gatekeepers' who can sift, sort, test, reproduce, document and then share. And this all takes a lot of time.

Three Questions

Try this simple exercise with your team.

Ask them to work in groups to answer three 'simple' questions:

1. Why don't we do lessons learned?
2. Why we should do lessons learned?
3. How can we do lessons learned?

Spend just ten minutes on each question, a quick sharing of ideas and then on to the next question.

Summarise the thoughts and then consider what to do to.

Overcome the obstacles to lessons learned being completed (assuming that you get a good number of reasons why your organisation should carry them out, of course).

Here are some examples of what you might gather from this exercise:

Question1: Why don't we do lessons learned?

- Too much effort
- No time
- Focused on 'doing' and not 'delivering'
- No clear benefit
- Apathy
- No way to share

- Project team have 'gone' already
- No workable process
- Lack of supportive culture
- Lack of facilitation/experience
- Blame culture
- Previous sessions not actioned
- Next project started
- Conflict potential
- Lack of perceived importance – peers/management
- Not mandated
- Advertises 'failures' as opposed to project 'success'

Question 2: Why we should do lessons learned?

- Avoid repeating same mistakes
- Builds a learning culture
- Fresh start/clear the air
- Improve efficiency
- Build trust, rapport and loyalty
- Stimulate innovation and creativity
- Improved quality and collaboration
- Shared understanding
- Honesty
- Improved project competency and process
- Confidence for future
- Promotes trust

Question 3: How can we do lessons learned?

- Build-in to project process/method/framework
- Plan in project schedule
- Incentivise project manager and team
- No 'blame' culture
- Management support
- Ensure emphasis is balanced – positive as well as 'improvements'
- Ensuring follows up actions are actioned
- Agile/iterative 'lessons learned' – don't wait until end of project
- External facilitation

Simple

So how do you get round all of this? Well one piece of advice is to keep it simple.

Well, we have already seen how one organisation approached this problem, in the Risk chapter.

Realising the real limitations of how to share the knowledge that they had and the nature of the majority of project managers, this organisation asked the project community to name one thing that would help them the most in this area and the response was 'risk'.

They mandated that one lesson learned was to be recorded and shared at the end of every project, and that was the biggest, unexpected issue that they encountered and what action they took to deal with this issue.

This was updated regularly and inserted into their in-house methodology tool and was, as a result, used (and updated because project managers saw the value).

Simple.

Notes

1 Milan Zeleny was a Czechoslovakian-American economist and a professor of management systems at Fordham University, New York City. He has done research in the field of decision-making, productivity, knowledge management and business economics.
2 AI will help with this.
3 Ai will help with this.
4 Ai will definitely help with this.

Going retro

Where we definitely don't look back in anger but look forward through the rear-view mirror and thereby avoid the onset of madness.

Unknowns

There is so much to learn at the end of any project and the ideal way to do this is through a retrospective. If you think that you know everything that went on during the project then you are simply mistaken, you don't honestly think that your project team told you everything do you? Of course they didn't.

But now is great time to uncover all of those 'known unknowns' and 'unknown unknowns' that are just out of your current understanding.

As noted, one of the best reference books for this activity is *Project Retrospectives* by Norman L Kerth[1]. I love the prime directive that Kerth governs his retrospectives by: "Regardless of what we discover, we must understand and truly believe that everyone did the best job he or she could, given what was known at the time, his or her skills and abilities, the resources available and the situation at hand".

There are treasures out there. No single person knows all there is to know about the project, and certainly not you, the project manager.

So go mining, there are nuggets of gold if only we pay attention and give ourselves the opportunity to uncover them. At least one of your project team will tell you something that will aid you in the future, and let you be a little more efficient. And the best way to make this happen is to plan for it to happen, right back at the very beginning of the project.

As part of this retrospective process make sure that you also take the opportunity to ask questions that you want answering. Remember? The things that you know what you don't know, the gaps in your experience on the project, the questions should ask your team.

Complete your knowledge by having an open and honest dialogue with the team. It may surprise them what you don't know, and they will most likely be pleased that they were able to help out during the project delivery.

DOI: 10.4324/9781003506522-67

Remember as a result of this activity:

* You still know what you know
* You also now know what you didn't know and now have received answers on the gaps in your knowledge hopefully
* You also now know what you didn't know you knew, through feedback from the team and other sources
* And, through the retrospective, you at least know a little more about what you didn't know that you didn't know – if the team have been very open with you

Timing

One of the keys to a successful retrospective is to wait... if you try and run one at the very end of the project, then there will all sorts of high emotions, celebrations, stresses, strains and residual tensions. Wait. Wait maybe one month after the project close, and then gather the team once more to join with you in the retrospective.

It is important that when you do re-group there is just an appreciation that you are all a bunch of people who tried to make a difference and deliver a successful project. There should be no structures, no hierarchy, no senior or junior members of the organisation or project at this point – just some people, who tried to make a difference, through a project.

Fun

A good retrospective should be a lot of fun, as well as a valuable learning experience. No PowerPoint and no lectures or reports, just a bunch of activities that require flipchart paper and coloured pens and post-it notes, an open mind and a sense of team spirit.

If run well then it will be looked back upon as a 'day well spent' by everyone who was involved and will be referred to by many people many times in the future.

Facilitator

One of the critical requirements for a successful retrospective is the involvement of a facilitator, an objective person who understands projects, understands the process and value of running a retrospective and who can get a group of people to open up and share.

The danger of using someone from within the project team is that they come with 'baggage' from the project delivery period and will already have preconceived ideas and opinions. The resulting retrospective will not be as 'open' or honest.

Value

It is important to understand the value of the retrospective and to 'sell' this value to everyone involved. As part of the planning for the retrospective the engaged facilitator should gather that this organisation is looking for in order that the correct agenda and workshop exercises are planned. It is possible to select multiple goals.

To aid this appreciation of value you can use the following 'value add' propositions:

- A retrospective review is an in-depth discussion that happens after the completion of a project
- It is structured to help the people involved reflect on the project in detail
- Its purpose is to learn from the experience of the recent project
- No one knows the whole story of the project rather each person involved has knowledge to share
- It is the collective telling of the story and mining the experience for knowledge and understanding to aid future projects

The deliverables of performing the retrospective are summarised as:

- A collective understanding of what happened and why
- Actionable lists: what to do differently next time, lessons learned, what worked well and topics for further discussion
- New insight added to the project knowledge inside the project team and the organisation
- Repaired damage to a project team (if this is relevant)
- Acknowledgment and appreciation of accomplishments

Potential goals could be:

- Uncover the real story

  - During any project no one person knows everything that went on and no one person knows how all of the pieces fit together, the whole story needs to be shared in an open and honest environment for everyone to understand each aspect and experience

- Improve upon the process, procedures, management and the culture

  - By looking back at what has occurred during the project then things that might be done differently and better the next time around can be identified, and the things that worked well and we want to repeat can also be confirmed

- Capture collective knowledge

    - By capturing the knowledge of the full team it becomes knowledge that is carried on by the team members (there remains a challenge on how that knowledge is disseminated to a wider audience of interested people but who out outside this particular project team and this is explored in the previous chapter 'Lessons Learned')

- Enjoy the success

    - A retrospective provides a wonderful opportunity for everyone to step back and appreciate what they have jointly managed to achieve

A further goal can be to build bridges among team members who have been stressed during the project period, might have fallen out with each, who still perhaps hold some sort of grudge or issue with a colleague. If this is the case, then the facilitator needs to be made aware of this and they can guide the sessions accordingly.

To validate the 'buy in' for the retrospective and for the facilitator to prepare for the retrospective, then ask the following questions:

- What would you like to accomplish by having this retrospective?
- What would a successful retrospective look like to you?
- What would you like to see happen after the retrospective?
- What are your greatest fears about this retrospective?
- What topics need to be addressed?
- What topics do I need to be careful with and why?
- What people do you wish to attend the retrospective?
- What details about the people can you share that I should know?

Needs

For a retrospective the following are the required materials:

- A suitable room for all of the attendees to work in and move around for the workshops. The room should allow for groups of five to work together
- Laptop projector: only for the short introduction to the retrospective, the rest of the day will not use PowerPoint at all
- At least two flip-chart stands with pads: ideally one flipchart for each group of five attendees
- Masking tape/Blu-tack to fix flipchart sheets to the wall: there must be room to do this on the wall of the room being used, as many of the exercises require attendees to work on them

- Marker pens in a variety of colours, with at least one pen for each person
- Post-it notes (six pads)
- Name tags: hopefully everyone will know each other by now but this is not always the case
- Digital camera: to record moments that should be remembered

Exercises

There is not fixed agenda as such for a retrospective but here are some exercises that work well:

Introductions

It is possible that some team members are meeting face to face for the first time. I this is the case there will be a need for formal and informal introductions to be made.

Remember my favourite 'ice-breaker' – it is a winner each time, trust me.

5 minutes of Fame

Each team member has to stand up in front of the team and has his five minutes of fame. They can use that time to focus in on a particular issue or something that they are most concerned about from the project delivery period. When their five minutes are over, the team can start a discussion on that immediately or the facilitator can record the key point and move on to the next team member for their five minutes of fame.

The team members do need to think about this and so, at the start of the retrospective, they should be given ten minutes or so to think about this, before the group begins to share.

Thanks

Each participant gets a 'gift', which they can give to a team member as appreciation for their work.

The gift can be chocolates, a flower, a voucher/coupon or anything small – it is not the gift itself that matters but the giving and the recognition. This is a great way to get your team closer together and to visualise gratitude for a 'job well done'.

Just imagine

Ask the team "When you think of this project, what image comes into your mind?" and then get them to draw that image. This can be done individually or in small groups (maximum of five) depending on the overall group numbers.

Once completed share with the group and then fix to the wall for later reference (capture these with the camera as well).

Define success

Ask the following of the group:

Was a definition of success for this project defined during project start-up? If so, then get them to reproduce that definition in some form.

If there was no definition of the project's success, then get the team to write a definition of success for the project now as they see it. Once this is done, again in smaller groups if appropriate, share that definition with the whole group.

Finally, as a whole group, decide if this project was a success according to the definition (the reproduced original definition if there was one or the newly defined one if not).

Timeline

This is best done on a large piece of paper – four or five sheets of flipchart paper affixed to the wall provides the best canvas to work on.

In the middle of the sheet, draw a timeline from left to right representing the start and the finish of the project. Draw a second line in the middle of the paper now – this will represent the 'emotional experience' later on – and mark this '+' (positive) at the top and '-' (negative) at the bottom.

Now break the timeline into segments that retrospective members will understand – dates, method phases, deliverables, milestones, etc.

Now get the participants put their notes of the significant events they remember from the project on the timeline at the approximate time when they happened.

Discuss the timeline with the group adding more notes as needed for the timeline to fully represent what happened and when it happened.

Emotional seismograph

Give each member a different coloured pen and get them to draw a continuous line on the chart of the project lifecycle, from the beginning of their involvement until the end of their involvement in the project (i.e., not everyone will have been with the project from the very start all the way until the end).

What this line should represent should be how each team member felt at each stage of the project, while they were involved, positive 'this is great' 'loving this project' 'we are on to a winner here' all the way down to a 'this is awful' 'why did I get involved in this' 'I am hating every moment, when will it end?, and some emotions in between.

The common view

Once the timeline and the emotional seismograph are completed, then the facilitator can lead a review and discussion asking such questions as:

What worked that we should do next time, and the time after that...?

What didn't work that we need to change somehow?

This should be recorded somewhere, possibly on the timeline sheet itself.

Finally, it is important to record 'what did the group learn' and to document 'what actions should be taken to maximise the profit from this experience.

Report

Once the day is over, there will be a need for a summary report and next actions to be prepared, and this should fall to the facilitator.

Best advice here is to utilise the visual imagery of the day by incorporating the photos that would have been taken during each of the exercises and annotating them with the key learning points and agreed actions.

When I am speaking on this retrospective subject, I like to offer up a practical example of an emotional experience, and it goes something like this:

On a large piece of paper – four or five sheets of flipchart paper affixed to the wall provides the best canvas to work on - in the middle of the sheet draw a timeline from left to right representing the start and the finish of the project or process or experience.

Now draw a second line in the middle of the paper - this will represent the 'emotional experience' later on – and mark this '+' (positive) at the top and '-' (negative) at the bottom.

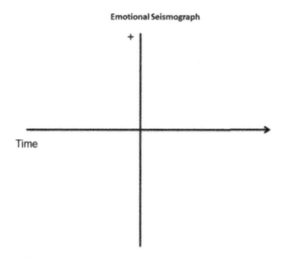

Figure 9.5.1 Emotional seismograph template.

Now imagine that you were coming to a presentation by Peter Taylor, The Lazy Project Manager. Perhaps you have heard good things from other people or this appeared to be an interesting subject matter – The Art of Productive Laziness, for example[2].

Your mood is high. But it is the time before the presentation and you are thinking that you do have a lot of work to do, and maybe this would be a better use of your time, but 'no', you will go as planned and listen to what Peter has to say. Your mood is still high, not as high as when you booked a few weeks ago, but high enough.

And then you arrive at the event, and Peter starts to talk, and you know what, he isn't quite as interesting as you first thought, or hoped he would be. Your mood is dropping.

He is going on about Italian economist and field-marshals in the Prussian army, dinosaurs and Monty Python. This is really not good at all. Your mood is now negative and dropping fast.

But it is getting towards the end of the presentation, at least Peter is running out of time, and so your mood rises back up into the positive.

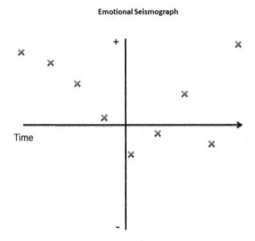

Figure 9.5.2 Emotional seismograph, example 1.

But oh, my goodness Peter has now opened a second PowerPoint presentation with 167 slides. You will be here forever. Your life is over.

And then he stops talking, you can escape and go and get a drink. Your mood is high once again.

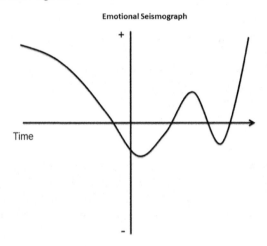

Figure 9.5.3 Emotional seismograph, example 2.

This therefore is your emotional experience of the presentation (I do hope that nobody really has this experience of course), but one thing is for sure – this is not my experience.

Mine goes like this.

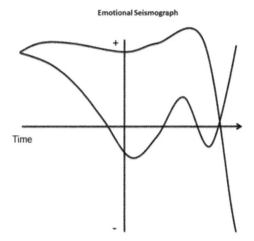

Figure 9.5.4 Emotional seismograph, example 3.

Hey, I am speaking to another new group of people in another exotic location somewhere around the world where I haven't been to yet (like Iceland and Hawaii – hint, hint[3]), and look at all of their smiley happy faces. They are loving everything that I have to say, they will all be lazy project managers in the future, and they might even buy a copy of my book *The Lazy Project Manager* (available from all good book retailers and online stores such as Amazon or from my own website at www.thelazyprojectmanager. com), and now I have run out of time, and I have to stop talking, and I am so depressed…

As you can see, my emotional experience is very different from yours – but why?

That is the key to understanding what the issues are. Why at the mid-point of the presentation was I, the speaker, so very positive, and yet you, the audience, so miserable? What needs to change, and what lessons can I learn to improve future presentations?

Notes

1 Project Retrospectives: A Handbook for Team Reviews by Norman L. Kerth, published by Dorset House Publishing: ISBN: 978-0-932633-44-6 - With detailed scenarios, imaginative illustrations, and step-by-step instructions, consultant and speaker Norman L. Kerth guides readers through productive, empowering retrospectives of project performance.
2 Many other presentation topics are offered of course including the option to commission a completely new customised presentation to suit your event.
3 OK blatant begging – I want to speak in Iceland, Hawaii would nice, love to go back to Dubai, Vancouver is on my list, Cape Town again … so many, so please get in touch, wherever you are.

A project manager's tale of escape without cause

One final story, and again, I am the project manager in question, much to my shame.

For the most part, I have really enjoyed all of my projects. That is not to say that there haven't been challenges over the years; high points and low points, moments when I felt that I had had enough, but equally good moments that I wanted to never end.

This tale is of a project within a manufacturing company that had a lot more low points than high points.

The project was 'challenging' (and it seemed close to impossible at times), the steering committee were 'difficult' (to say the least), the project team were 'mixed' in their interest and capability (to put it mildly), and I was a long way from home. The entire experience really tested me as a project manager pretty much from day one, but I felt that I had acquitted myself in a good way. In a good way until the very end of the project, that is.

So, to quickly move to the point of this story, the project reached a conclusion. The deliverables were delivered, and the company reluctantly agreed to signing off the project. The job was done.

Except it wasn't.

I had had quite a hellish experience over the months and just wanted it all to come to an end. And so, when that final steering committee meeting was done and the minutes signed off, I have to admit that I almost ran to my car, jumped in and tore out of the car park deliriously happy. The motorway home called to me and, with some rock music blaring out of the speakers[1], I decided to write this one off to history and to never return again.

I was one happy project manager.

Then I was asked to go back and to a post-project review!

My heart sank, and I began to make up 101 reasons why I was too busy, too sick, too mentally incompetent, too 'about to go on a spontaneous holiday' and too 'I just don't want to go back' to, well, avoid going back.

I didn't go back. Someone else did.

And so that was that.

DOI: 10.4324/9781003506522-68

Except it wasn't. My inquisitiveness eventually got the better of me, and I sat down with the other project manager, sometime after the review, and I discovered many things that I had never known about my own project.

I discovered (obviously through this other project manager) that the company had had a very bad experience in a similar previous project and, as a result, they were nervous about this project. Very nervous indeed.

I discovered that the project had been strongly championed by one of the steering members despite a lot of resistance from others in the business, and a lot – their reputation and possibly career, for example – depended upon a successful outcome.

I discovered that two people on the project team had, shall we say, personal 'issues' during the early part of the project, and this led to some residual tension between them.

I discovered that there was felt to be a 'black hole' in one particular business area where the purpose and benefit, the justification, of the project was never explained.

I discovered that they thought that I was a very strong and competent project manager, but one who focused perhaps not enough on the human side of the project.

And I personally discovered – and I did not have to be told this by my project management colleague – that I had missed a great deal by leaving the project before its final conclusion.

I personally discovered that I should have stayed for the full and proper closure. I would have learnt so much.

Note

1 More than likely some Black Sabbath.

Chapter 10

Productivity – Destination

Concluding the personal productivity journey, we reflect on the path of personal change and growth, likening it to a navigation system guiding one from point 'A' to point 'B'. We emphasise the importance of starting the journey and equally acknowledge that each individual's destination is unique, depending on their ambitions and goals. Drawing parallels to the reliability of satellite navigation, we highlight the benefits of having a calm and assured leader in guiding one's path towards success.

Furthermore, we consider the warning against blindly following instructions without understanding or internalising them. Through a cautionary tale about a fisherman content with his simple life, we underscore the value of prioritising personal fulfillment and balance over relentless pursuit of external success. Encouraging all readers to learn from the guidance provided but ultimately make their own decisions and adaptations on the journey towards becoming the best version of themselves.

DOI: 10.4324/9781003506522-69

Destination

You have reached your destination

Only you will know what your destination is, based on the work that you did at the earlier on. And, of course, all this will take some time – depending on your personal ambitions and productivity goals.

Have you at least started out on the journey?

I joked that you could think of this book as the 'sat nav' for your journey for change.

Well, these days I use a satellite navigation system in my own car, actually I love Waze[1], but I realise other options are available on the market.

Not all of the time though, since it is not built into the old Saab[2] that I drive but has to be stuck on the windscreen and connected to the power from the lighter socket. So '2006' I know, but that's just the way it is. It's my car, and I love it.

But it is a comfort, and I do enjoy the calm, unruffled and dispassionate advice that she hands out to me by voice and by graphical display.

The days of map-reading and general direction guidance was an instant recipe for marital strife since neither the driver nor the guide could ever agree on the need for information, the speed of supply of this information, the accuracy of the information, or anything really. A simple trip to a new location for a convivial lunch with relatives or the delivery of a small child to the house of a new friend could escalate the likelihood of divorce proceedings being initiated as easily as match ignites dynamite.

These days it is so much better. My Waze asks me where I want to go, and when, and then breaks the route down into small steps or stages and off we go. The great thing is that when Waze is wrong (I do occasionally obviously know better than her and her satellite friend), and I drive past the turning she politely asked me to take, she quietly acknowledges my superior intelligence with the phrase 'recalculating' and then gives me the right directions. She can be wrong but just appreciates the lessons learned and recalculates.

DOI: 10.4324/9781003506522-70

Conversely, the mere hint that I might not manage to take that sharp left that was announced to me a massive 25 metres before the actual turning by my human navigator can result in three weeks of subsequent marital silence.

So it is clear to me that it is the calm and assured leader who gets you from 'A' to 'B' in the most effective way.

Now, great as my 'sat nav' can be, it has one huge drawback. If I follow the instructions once to find my 'B', then I will most likely not be able to find it a second time through my own devices. I will need Waze the second time as well, and the third.

Following instructions blindly teaches you nothing.

I will need a guide each and every time unless I look up and do it myself at some point.

"If you always do what you always did, you'll always get what you always got".[3]

The real art here is to learn what you need to learn and then make it your own. It is your 'change', your 'journey', your 'life', so take what you need from this book and adapt it all to turn yourself into the 'winner' that you want to be – the lazy winner hopefully.

A cautionary tale

A man was on vacation and was standing at the pier of a small island village when a small boat with just one fisherman docked.

Inside the small boat were several large groupers. The man complimented the islander on the quality of his fish and asked how long it took to catch them.

The islander replied: "Only a little while".

The man considered for a while and then asked the fisherman why didn't he stay out longer and catch more fish?

The islander said he had enough to support his family's immediate needs.

The man then thought some more before he asked, "But what do you do with the rest of your time?"

The fisherman said, "I sleep late, fish a little, play with my children, take a late afternoon nap with my wife, stroll into the village each evening where I sip rum and play guitar with my friends. I have a full and busy life".

The man scoffed at this answer and said, "I am a professional man with an MBA and many years of experience, and I could help you".

The fisherman looked puzzled and asked the man how he could help.

"You should spend more time fishing and, with the proceeds, buy a bigger boat. Then with the proceeds from the bigger boat you could buy several boats. Eventually you would have a fleet of fishing boats. Instead of selling your catch to a middleman, you would sell directly to the processor, eventually opening your own cannery.

You would control the product, processing and distribution. You would, of course, need to leave this small fishing village and move to the city to run your expanding enterprise", declared the man with authority.

The fisherman asked, "But, how long will this all take?"

To which the man replied, "About fifteen to twenty years should do it, I think".

"But what then?", asked the fisherman.

The man laughed and said that this was the best part. "When the time is right you would sell your company stock to the public and become very rich, you would make millions".

"Millions, really? Then what?", questioned the villager.

The man thought for a short while and said, "Then you would retire. Move to a small fishing village where you would sleep late, fish a little, play with your kids, take a late afternoon nap with your wife, stroll to the village in the evenings. Here you could sip rum and play your guitar with your friends".

The fisherman smiled at the man and took his catch home.

The man stood looking confused for a while before he walked away from the pier.

Notes

1 Waze Mobile Ltd, doing business as Waze, formerly FreeMap Israel, is a subsidiary company of Google that provides satellite navigation software on smartphones and other computers that support the Global Positioning System.
2 It actually was a Saab 9-3 Aero convertible, but I also have a Range Rover for sensible journeys.
3 Source unknown.

Chapter 11

AI Magic

We cannot ignore the rise of Artificial Intelligence (AI) and here we look into the initial perceptions and practical applications of AI in project management. Opening with a debunking of common AI myths, contrasting popular culture references like Terminator with real-world examples such as the UK Patent Office's challenge.

Transitioning to the project management domain, we (hopefully) can seamlessly integrate AI into existing practices, drawing parallels with the evolution of navigation tools like Waze. Just as such tools augment a drivers' abilities by providing real-time guidance, AI promises to streamline project management processes, enabling professionals to work smarter, not harder.

Looking ahead, visions of a future where AI-enabled efficiency revolutionises project management, akin to the promise of autonomous vehicles for safer and more enjoyable journeys. We conclude with a call to embrace AI as a valuable ally in driving project success, underscoring the importance of focusing on people amid technological advancements.

DOI: 10.4324/9781003506522-71

AI – the starting point

When the term "Artificial Intelligence[1]" is mentioned, it's not uncommon for references to Terminator or Skynet to come up, conjuring images of a dystopian future. However, the reality of AI is far from the apocalyptic scenarios portrayed in movies. Take, for example, the UK Patent Office, which has been granting patents since the 15th century. Recently, there was a case known as the Davis hearing decision, where an attempt was made to file a patent for an invention created by AI. This raised important questions about whether non-human entities could be considered inventors. While the application was rejected, it sparked a conversation about the role of AI in innovation and the need for future consideration.

However, AI's current capabilities can sometimes be quirky and even amusing, as highlighted in a TED talk by AI researcher Janelle Shane. She explores the peculiar behaviours of AI algorithms as they attempt to solve human problems, such as creating new ice cream flavours or distinguishing between human fingers and fish. Despite its limitations and occasional absurdities, AI has the potential to revolutionise project management practices in the near future.

As we embrace the inevitability of AI's integration into various industries, including project management, it's essential to remain optimistic about its potential benefits.

Arthur C. Clarke declared that "Any sufficiently advanced technology is indistinguishable from magic", which we should take into account as we embrace this new world of AI-aided project management.

AI has the power to enhance project management by offering independent thinking, creativity, compassion and collaboration. By leveraging AI technologies, project managers can expect to navigate projects more efficiently and effectively, ultimately leading to greater success. Therefore, rather than fearing the unknown, we should embrace AI as a tool that will empower us to excel in our professional endeavours.

DOI: 10.4324/9781003506522-72

Note

1 Artificial Intelligence (AI) emerged in the 1950s, focusing on the theory and advancement of computer systems capable of mimicking human intelligence in tasks like visual perception, speech recognition, decision-making and language translation. Machine Learning, a branch of AI and computer science originating in the 1990s, involves training algorithmic models with existing data to enable them to make decisions or predictions. Deep Learning, which gained prominence in the 2010s, employs layered neural networks to analyse data and make informed decisions, constituting a subset of machine learning techniques. Generative AI, a development of the 2020s, harnesses algorithmic models to generate new content, encompassing written, visual and auditory mediums, often prompted by existing data or user inputs.

11.2

AI and the Project Manager

I had the pleasure of writing a book about the topic and with the specific view of waking up my profession to what was heading our way (fast).

AI and the Project Manager: How the Rise of Artificial Intelligence Will Change Your World[1] was released in 2021, and, at the time, mine was rare voice in project management. I am very pleased to say that this is no longer the case, and everything seems to be about artificial intelligence.

In 2009 I wrote, as part of the introduction to *The Lazy Project Manager*, as follows:

"Productive laziness is all about success, but success with far less effort. By advocating being a 'lazy' project manager, I do not intend that we should all do absolutely nothing. I am not saying we should all sit around drinking coffee, reading good books, and engaging in idle gossip whilst watching the project hours go by and the non-delivered project milestones disappear over the horizon. That would obviously be just plain stupid and would result in an extremely short career in project management – in fact, probably in a very short career, full stop!

Lazy does not mean stupid.

No, I really mean that we should all adopt a more focused approach to project management and exercise our efforts where it really matters, rather than rushing around like busy, busy bees involving ourselves in unimportant, non-critical activities that others can better address, or which do not need addressing at all in some cases.

Welcome to the home of 'productive laziness'".

You will recognise this as exactly the same sentiment that is at the start of this book, because my views have not changed.

Personally, and I quite sure most project managers would agree, anything that can alleviate some of the repetitive and arduous (but important of course) tracking, analytics and reporting activities, and not only alleviate but improve, then sign me up!

DOI: 10.4324/9781003506522-73

Note

1   *AI and the Project Manager: How the Rise of Artificial Intelligence Will Change Your World* - Routledge 28 Oct 2021.

AI driving

Let's view the integration of AI into project management through a car analogy. Consider navigating through a complex city like London. In the past, options were limited: either you mastered "The Knowledge[1]" like London taxi drivers, or you relied on tools like Waze for real-time guidance.

"The Knowledge" exemplifies human expertise, requiring rigorous training to understand every nook and cranny of the city's roads. Conversely, Waze represents AI-powered navigation, leveraging collaborative data to optimise routes dynamically. It's a shift from memorisation to real-time adaptability, freeing drivers to focus on the road.

Similarly, project management faces a transition. While full autonomy may not be imminent, AI promises significant enhancements. Just as Waze augments drivers' abilities, AI can streamline project management processes, empowering professionals to work smarter, not harder. By embracing AI, project managers can focus on core responsibilities like team management, while algorithms handle repetitive tasks and optimise workflows.

The future of project management lies in AI-enabled efficiency. Just as autonomous vehicles promise safer and more enjoyable journeys, AI-driven project management holds the potential to revolutionise how projects are delivered. As we usher in this new era, let's welcome AI as a valuable ally in driving project success and embracing the principles of working smarter, not harder.

There are certainly a number of areas that AI could partner up with a project manager:

- Resource Allocation: AI will be able to assess project requirements, team availability, and skillsets to optimise resource allocation – the right people – the right tasks – right time.
- Risk Management: AI algorithms will be capable of looking at historical project data, identify potential risks and predict future risks based on patterns, enabling project managers to develop proactive risk-mitigation strategies.

DOI: 10.4324/9781003506522-74

- Scheduling and Planning: AI-powered tools will rapidly create accurate and detailed project schedules optimising project timelines and ensuring the efficient use of critical resources.
- Task Automation: AI will allow for automatic repetitive and time-consuming tasks such as data entry, reporting, and documentation, freeing up project managers and team members to focus on higher-value activities, like people motivation and leadership.
- Predictive Analytics: By analysing historical project data, AI will be able to provide insights into project performance and predict project outcomes, as well as identifying areas for improvement.
- Stakeholder Management: AI-powered chatbots and virtual assistants can support project managers in communicating with stakeholders, providing timely updates, answering queries, and facilitating collaboration.
- Quality Assurance: AI algorithms will be able to analyse project deliverables, detect defects or deviations from any recorded standards, and recommend corrective actions to ensure the quality of project outcomes.
- Cost Estimation and Budgeting: AI can delve into the data around project requirements, historical cost data, and market trends in order to generate more accurate and up to the minute cost estimates and budgets, enabling project managers to plan and allocate resources effectively.
- Document Management: AI-powered document management systems will be able to organise, categorise and search project-related documents, making it easier for project teams to access relevant information and collaborate much faster and more efficiently.
- Decision Support: AI will offer the ability to provide decision support to project managers by analysing complex datasets, identifying patterns, and recommending optimal courses of actions, thereby enhancing the decision-making process throughout the project lifecycle.

My advice is to explore and discover what is out there and certainly do not be passive. I smile when I read "you won't lose your job to AI, but you will lose your job to someone who adopts AI".

Get active!

Note

1 The London taxicab driver is required to be able to decide routes immediately in response to a passenger's request or traffic conditions, rather than stopping to look at a map, relying on satellite navigation or asking a controller by radio. Consequently, the "Knowledge of London" is the in-depth study of a number of pre-set London street routes and all places of interest that taxicab drivers in that city must complete to obtain a licence to operate a black cab. It was initiated in 1865 and has changed little since. It is the world's most demanding training course for taxicab drivers, and applicants will usually need to pass at least 12 'appearances' (periodical one-on-one oral examinations undertaken throughout the qualification process), with the whole process averaging 34 months to pass.

Don't be a DIKW

The DIKW model, which stands for Data, Information, Knowledge and Wisdom, is a hierarchy often used to understand how raw data transforms into valuable insights and informed decisions. In the context of AI, this model can be applied to illustrate how AI systems process and utilise data to provide knowledge guidance for people, such as project managers.

Data: At the base of the DIKW pyramid is data, which refers to raw, unprocessed facts and figures without any inherent meaning. In AI, data is the foundational input, encompassing vast amounts of text, images, audio, and other forms of unstructured and structured data. AI systems ingest this data through various sensors, databases and input mechanisms.

Information: Once data is collected, AI systems process it to extract information, which is data that has been organized and given context. For instance, a natural language processing model can take raw text data and identify patterns, categorise content and extract key phrases. Information provides a more coherent structure that can be interpreted and utilised for specific purposes.

Knowledge: Knowledge emerges when information is further processed and analyzed to draw meaningful insights. AI systems, particularly those utilising machine learning and deep learning algorithms, can detect trends, make predictions and recognise complex patterns that may not be apparent through simple analysis. For example, in healthcare, AI can analyse patient data to identify potential diagnoses and recommend treatments based on historical data and clinical research. Here, the AI acts as a knowledge provider, offering guidance based on a comprehensive analysis of available information.

Wisdom: The pinnacle of the DIKW model is wisdom, which involves making informed decisions and taking actions based on the accumulated knowledge. While AI itself may not possess wisdom in the human sense, it can support human decision-makers by providing actionable insights and recommendations. In business, AI-driven analytics can guide strategic

DOI: 10.4324/9781003506522-75

decisions, optimise operations and personalise customer experiences, effectively translating knowledge into practical wisdom.

So actually, I mean to be a 'DIKW' but know that the wisdom aspect must come from the human partnership.

In summary, the DIKW model applied to AI demonstrates the progression from raw data to actionable insights. AI systems enhance this process by efficiently processing vast amounts of data, transforming it into useful information, extracting valuable knowledge and guiding decisions that embody wisdom. This capability positions AI as a crucial tool for knowledge guidance across various domains.

There may be trouble ahead

As we have seen in the future, the integration of AI into project management holds the promise of significant benefits, including enhanced efficiency, streamlined processes and data-driven decision-making. AI-powered tools will empower project managers to allocate resources more effectively, optimize project timelines, and mitigate risks more proactively. By automating repetitive tasks and offering valuable insights derived from vast datasets, AI will enable project teams to focus on strategic priorities, fostering innovation and driving project success.

However, alongside these benefits come some inherent risks that must be carefully managed.

The reliance on AI-driven solutions raises concerns regarding data privacy, security vulnerabilities, and potential biases in algorithmic decision-making. As AI becomes increasingly intertwined with project management practices, it is essential to prioritise transparency, accountability and ethical considerations. Proactive measures, such as robust cybersecurity protocols, ongoing training for AI algorithms and regular audits of AI systems, will be essential to mitigate these risks and ensure that AI remains a force for positive change in project management.

DOI: 10.4324/9781003506522-76

Top tips for getting AI empowered

Think along these lines when you are getting ready, or your company is getting ready, to embrace the AI empowered project world.

Wise words to remember are that AI may not replace you, but AI will definitely change the way you work.

And get involved in your local project community, team, chapter, group (whatever) because the chances are close to 100 per cent that they are battling on the same journey as you want to undertake.

- Define Clear Objectives: Clearly define the objectives and goals you want to achieve by adopting AI in project management. Whether it's improving efficiency, reducing costs, or enhancing decision-making, having clear objectives will guide your AI implementation strategy.
- Understand AI Technologies: Familiarise yourself with different AI technologies and their applications in project management. Understand how machine learning, natural language processing, predictive analytics and other AI techniques can be leveraged to address specific project challenges.
- Start Small, Scale Gradually: Begin by implementing AI solutions in small, manageable areas of your project management processes. Start with pilot projects or proof-of-concepts to test the effectiveness of AI technologies before scaling up across the organisation.
- Data Quality and Accessibility: Ensure that you have access to high-quality data that is relevant, accurate and up to date. Clean and organise your data to maximise the effectiveness of AI algorithms in generating insights and predictions.
- Collaboration and Training: Foster a culture of collaboration and continuous learning within your project team. Provide training and support to team members to help them understand how AI tools work and how they can leverage them to improve their workflows.

DOI: 10.4324/9781003506522-77

- Integration with Existing Systems: Integrate AI solutions seamlessly with your existing project management systems and workflows. Ensure compatibility and interoperability with tools such as project management software, collaboration platforms and data repositories.
- Monitor and Evaluate Performance: Regularly monitor the performance of AI algorithms and solutions to ensure they are delivering the expected outcomes. Evaluate key performance indicators (KPIs) such as accuracy, efficiency and return on investment to measure the success of your AI initiatives.
- Ethical and Legal Considerations: Consider the ethical and legal implications of using AI in project management, especially regarding data privacy, security, bias and transparency. Ensure compliance with relevant regulations and industry standards.
- Iterate and Improve: Continuously iterate and improve your AI implementation based on feedback and lessons learned. Stay updated with the latest advancements in AI technology and best practices in project management to stay ahead of the curve.
- Embrace Change: Embrace the changes that AI brings to project management processes and workflows. Be open to exploring new possibilities and adapting to the evolving landscape of AI-driven project management.

Ask ChatGPT

I couldn't resist but to ask ChatGPT what it felt (probably the wrong word here) thought on being an AI empowered productively lazy project manager. This is what I got back (I think it closely aligns to my own thoughts, but interesting anyway):

A 'productively lazy' project manager would seek ways to automate repetitive tasks and streamline processes to maximise efficiency while minimising effort. Here's how such a project manager could use AI in their work:

- Automating Task Assignments: AI-powered project management tools can analyse team members' skills, workload and availability to automatically assign tasks, saving time and ensuring the right person is assigned to each job.
- Predictive Analytics for Resource Allocation: AI algorithms can analyse past project data to predict resource needs for future projects. This helps in allocating resources efficiently and avoiding over or underutilisation of team members.
- Smart Scheduling: AI can optimise project schedules by considering dependencies, resource availability and project constraints. This ensures that tasks are completed on time with minimal conflicts.

- Risk Management: AI can analyse project data to identify potential risks and suggest mitigation strategies. By proactively addressing risks, the project manager can prevent delays and cost overruns.
- Natural Language Processing (NLP): NLP-powered tools can parse and analyse project documentation, emails and other communication channels to extract relevant information, such as action items or risks, automatically updating project plans and status reports.
- Chatbots for Team Support: AI-powered chatbots can answer common questions from team members, freeing up the project manager's time for more strategic activities.
- Quality Assurance: AI can analyse project deliverables to ensure they meet quality standards. For example, AI can perform code reviews or check design specifications for compliance.
- Performance Monitoring: AI algorithms can monitor project progress in real-time, identifying potential bottlenecks or deviations from the plan. This allows the project manager to intervene promptly and keep the project on track.

Keep on being realistically 'Lazy'

But all that said I truly believe that the Lazy Project Manager was built for the AI empowered project management world.

It's what we have all been waiting for, by using technology to find the easiest way to do something and to spend the freed-up time on focusing on people.

Because people deliver projects.

People!

Chapter 12

Multiple Laziness

Now the focus shifts to the challenge of managing multiple projects simultaneously, emphasising the importance of having a solid foundation in each project and the ability to delegate effectively to project teams.

We discuss the myth of multitasking, citing research that suggests individuals who pride themselves on multitasking often perform less efficiently. Continuing we investigate potential strategies for managing multiple projects, including having a 'safety valve' representative in each project and being conscious of your own personal style of project management, drawing an analogy to different roles in a music band.

Finally, various perspectives on the role of a project manager, ranging from a drummer to a vocalist, are explored, along with comparisons to other roles like project sponsor or roadie.

DOI: 10.4324/9781003506522-78

Being 'lazy' on more than one project at a time

Projects are generally getting more complex (or complicated – there is a difference) and that adds a challenge to today's project managers but what I more often hear from many project managers is that their particular challenge is that of multiple project responsibility.

I resonate with this issue as, when I ran projects, I would be typically looking after three or more at any given time, all at different stages in the project lifecycle.

It all helps add a dimension of extra 'fun' to the role of project manager, as well as an overlay of pressure.

But at the end of the day, success in this world still comes from the application of the dinosaur theory, as covered earlier in this very book.

Remember "The Lazy Project Manager's Theory of Projects, from a Productive Laziness aspect: All projects are thick at one end, much, much thinner in the middle and then thick again at the far end. That is the theory that I have, and which is mine, and what it is too".

If you have the right foundations in your projects, then multiple project management is not so difficult. It becomes difficult when you can't balance your time and efforts between the projects, and when you don't (or can't) delegate to your various project teams, where you spend the majority of your time in a reactive state rather than the correct proactive state.

Remember the second theory "If you want to get a brontosaurus from A to B then you ride the dinosaur – you don't carry it!"

Some people advise that to do this multiple focused work you should work in discrete periods of time each day on each one in turn. Others say that you should allocate 'x' amount of time per project and cycle through them throughout the week. Personally, what worked for me was that good foundation, and a good project team delegated and empowered. I would then, at the start of each day, assess what and who I needed to call or get an update on and start from there. There was no fixed cycle of project focus but only applying the good old 80/20 rule across all of the projects.

DOI: 10.4324/9781003506522-79

What also worked was being open and ready and having the time to react rapidly to any project issue that arose without impacting my other projects.

You should note that the ability to multi-task is not one of our true capabilities. In fact, according to a recent study[1], employees who pride themselves on being above average for multitasking capabilities are actually the very worst at carrying out their duties efficiently. According to University of Utah psychologists David Strayer and David Sanbonmatsu[2], people who identify as strong multitaskers tend to be impulsive, sensation-seeking, and overconfident in their ability to juggle multiple tasks simultaneously. In fact, note the researchers, the people who multitask the most are often the least capable of doing so effectively.

One last tip I would add. In each of your projects have a 'safety valve' representative, someone whose role it is (not a full-time role of course) challenge you, the project manager, if they are concerned about their project and have noticed an issue or significant pitfall that you are missing due to your multi-project management responsibility.

Notes

1 The study was performed on a sample of students of psychology at the University of Utah.
2 https://pubmed.ncbi.nlm.nih.gov/23372720.

What is your style?

You should also consider your own 'style' of project management. Music is a very personal matter; as I write this, I am listening to the band Golden Earring playing 'Radar Love' (perhaps the finest pop/rock single ever produced... see, you are already disagreeing with me, it is a personal choice after all, I know that). But musical taste aside, if you take a fairly typical four-piece pop/rock band, it commonly consists of a drummer, a bass player, a lead guitarist and a vocalist.

- The drummer provides a steady beat and emphasises the other instruments and vocals, perhaps with the occasional solo where they have full control of the flow and style of the music being played. The drummer can be very influential within a band.
- The bass player has the pivotal role in the band and the group members depend on the bassist's subtle lead. If the guitarist or drummer makes a mistake it can easily go unnoticed but if the bassist makes a mistake, everyone will instantly know that something is wrong.
- The lead guitarist is one of the most important contributors, whether they just add in riffs here and there or play mesmerising guitar solos. There is an added attraction to the role, in that they are typically second only to the lead vocalist when it comes to fame, spotlight and all that comes with that.
- Finally, the lead vocalist is most often the main focus of the audience's attention. This is due partly to the fact that, as front person, they interpret the lyrics which make up the story of the song, and due partly to the singer's charisma.

Now consider your style as a project manager. Which one are you?

- A 'drummer', offering a steady backbeat to keep the rhythm of the project on track?

DOI: 10.4324/9781003506522-80

- A 'bassist', keeping the team together and ensuring that no mistakes are made?
- A 'lead guitarist', adding in inspirational leadership moments and creativity?
- A 'vocalist', interpreting the vision of the project and being the figurehead?

Or perhaps you play more than one role ...

And maybe I should have added that the project sponsor is perhaps more like the band manager/impresario, although one person I spoke to added, "sadly I think the project sponsor can sometimes be more like the cynical musical journalist!".

Another person proposed that the project manager was the 'roadie', making sure that all aspects from start to end perform successfully.

And finally, a few wise words from a further commentator, who's more into classical music, "The conductor is like the project manager – he doesn't need to be able to play all the instruments, just to get the best out of the performers – the band/orchestra/project team".

Chapter 13

Quick Tips to Productive Lazy Heaven

Finally, if you did skip ahead then you are now helpfully advised on what you may have missed with a summary from bizarre anecdotes about dinosaurs to the application of the 'lazy' philosophy in various life scenarios.

We challenge you to consider whether the essence of the book's theory can be distilled down to just 20 per cent of its content for maximum productivity. Through a playful exploration of laziness and efficiency, you will be encouraged to test this theory and reflect on your own journey toward becoming 'productively lazy'.

Whether you arrived at this point eagerly or methodically, this serves as a reference for applying the principles of 'productive laziness' in future endeavours or as a gentle reminder to revisit the chapters they may have overlooked[1].

Note

1 And that the author laboured so heavily over.

DOI: 10.4324/9781003506522-81

Make it smaller

I'll take one of those, but do you have it in a smaller size, please?

What did I miss?

If you were among those who didn't cheat and read conscientiously through all the chapters, then you didn't miss anything; you can go straight to productive heaven with my blessing.

But if you did cheat then, hey, you missed a lot!

You missed something really interesting about eating dinosaurs, wearing ermine cloaks and how to spot a psychopathic woman at a funeral. We discovered the use for a creep'o'meter, learned why you should never go ballooning. We avoided a big red bus, learned how to deliver a good Oscar acceptance speech and appreciated why it is important for your team that you read the newspaper each morning. Oh, and we discovered a little something about mining for gold.

We may also have briefly mentioned project management.

But don't worry, it wasn't all that important. Don't feel you have to go all the way back just to catch up.

DOI: 10.4324/9781003506522-82

Take me to productive heaven now

So I guess the question is this: in order to learn to become productively lazy, with all the application of the science of laziness, the 80/20 rule, the lazy to smart ratio, and all that, can you, the reader, apply the lazy rule to the lazy learning curve in an even more lazy way and basically get up the lazy learning curve in a faster way?

Put it this way, out of everything I have mentioned in this book so far, does the very principle that is the essence behind the theory mean that only 20% of what has been covered in the previous pages is really, really critical in adapting your project management work style in order to achieve the productive lazy life? Can you sweat it a whole lot less in order to join me in the comfy chair?

An interesting theory. Shall we test it[1]?

Well, you will have arrived here in one of two ways. Directly, from the 'Can I cheat?' chapter – in which case you are most likely to be impatiently lazy with a desire for rapid productiveness, and that will be either a good thing or a foolhardy thing; only you and your mother can be the judge of that. Alternatively, you have progressed honestly and carefully through all the intervening chapters to arrive here in both a calm and fully prepared state. And that can only be a good thing; no need to involve your mother on this one.

Whichever, the following should be useful to you in several ways: for shortcutting the whole process and proving to yourself that you are already lazy and productive, as reference material for future application of the theory of productive laziness or possibly as proof to yourself that you need to go back and read all the chapters between 'Can I Cheat?' and this one since you don't have a clue what the following material is all about.

Let's see if it works. Ready?

OK, well, cutting out 80 per cent of the content of the learning points from the preceding chapters and focusing on the remaining 20 per cent gives something like this:

DOI: 10.4324/9781003506522-83

A project: thick at the start or initiation; no time for rest right now, work hard and rest later.

It is important for you to stay ahead of the game:	• Start as you mean to go on and be confident, as this does breed success. • Dress smartly and get the upper hand as soon as you can; stay on that moral high ground for as long as you can and always be prepared. • Anticipate everything you can and keep your eye on the end game so that you can drive the project in a direct manner towards conclusion and success.
You need to manage your sponsor	• So ask them what they expect from you and the project but do make sure you manage the first meeting and use the right questions and have an open discussion with them. • Apply the power grid to help you understand your sponsor better and appreciate the types of power that they may have. • Also appreciate that understanding what is in it for your sponsor will aid your ability to work with them. • Understand your own organisation and work out if there is a need to join the campaign for real project sponsorship.

And you need to manage the project creep:	• Creep is inevitable but there is nothing wrong with measuring the potential creepiness of the project team in order to be better prepared.
	• Manage the change process on your project and use the process immediately as a showcase and education for your team.
	• If you can't use the suggestion or request then park it in the parking lot – but don't forget it and thank contributors for their ideas, always.
You have to avoid surprises	• Learn from previous project experience.
	• Ensure your risk approach is appropriate and relevant to what might actually happen.
	• Ask yourself if you are the right project manager for this project and, if the answer isn't a wholehearted (and honest) 'yes' – get some help immediately.
You must avoid a communication breakdown at all costs	• You must communicate as others need you to communicate, understand how communication works and be honest and be open in your communication.
	• Effective but minimal communication is better than ineffective and overwhelming communication.
	• Appreciate that modern communication is both a benefit and a hindrance; communicate the communication plan to everyone and stress that reporting is not communicating.

A project: thin in the middle – do it right and this is where you could get to rest, at least some; do it wrong, and you will be busy all day, every day.

Thick at the end

Thick at the start

Have fun, it's all in a day's work and it will help the project along nicely	• So start with a smile and a joke and appreciate that you have to laugh to make fun part of your project. • But always practice safe fun, and don't offend anyone. • If you are smart with your people then fun will be an inherent part of your project and you won't have to do very much at all; just make sure that you end with a laugh and a wave.
Breathe normally at all times	• Stay calm in a crisis, and one way to do this is to get the planning right and not panic but just breathe normally when you do hit a problem. • Always filter, filter, filter then delegate, delegate, delegate and finally prioritise, prioritise, prioritise each and every problem that comes your way. • Breathe normally at all times in order to make the right decisions to keep the project on track.

Make sure that there is lot of 'lurve' in the room	• First, do the groundwork and make your project attractive to others. • Then get the best team that you can and feed the feel-good factor so that the team really feels that they are appreciated, and in the right way. • Consider whether it's nature or nurture that will make the feelgood factor thrive in this project; help yourself by spotting the carers you may have on the team and make sure that you analyse the love that each team member requires.
Give good feedback	• It is a tough thing to do well so learn what you need to learn. • Always address the problem and not the person. • Be realistic in what the outcomes could be.
It is OK for the lights to be on and no one at home, within reason	• So avoid swamping yourself with communication and demands for your time. • Have an open-door policy, but also be a good manager and control the open-door access. • Think about number one – you – for the greater good of the project team and keep analysing and reducing, where you need to, your involvement. Others may have better solutions or answers

A project: thick again at the end, so do some work here, it's worth it; don't rush to complete.

Thick at the end

Thick at the start

Search for the missing link in the project knowledge and history

- First, finish what you started, properly and thoroughly to the benefit of everyone.
- Then document what you know yourself about the project, find out what you don't know about the project and, without shame, ask others what you now need to know to have a fuller understanding.
- Learn the lessons that are there to be learned and share everything by telling others what you now know.

Be a better project manager (oh, and just ignore all that stuff about dinosaurs, cloaks, psychopaths, creep'o'meters, ballooning, buses, speeches, newspapers and gold – it will probably only confuse you).

But definitely, embrace the AI future of project management – be a leader, not a late arrival.

Note

1 There is 'Pareto' science behind this, by the way. Are you ready? OK, mathematically, where something is shared among a sufficiently large set of participants, there will always be a number k between 50 and 100, such that k% is taken by $(100 - k)$% of the participants; however, k may vary from 50 in the case of equal distribution (e.g. exactly 50% of the people take 50% of the resources) to nearly 100 in the case of a tiny number of participants taking almost all of the resources. There is nothing special about the number 80, but many systems will have k somewhere around this region of intermediate imbalance in distribution. This is a special case of the wider phenomenon of Pareto distributions. If the parameters in the Pareto distribution are chosen suitably, then one would have not only 80% of effects coming from 20% of causes, but also 80% of that top 80% of effects coming from 20% of that top 20% of causes, and so on (80% of 80% is 64%; 20% of 20% is 4%, so this implies a '64-4 law').

Chapter 14

Quick Tips to Personal Productivity Heaven

Now we try to make this as easy as possible in order to satisfy your now hunger to be productively lazy in everything you do, as well as helping others to be the same.

DOI: 10.4324/9781003506522-84

Size matters

You are now hereby challenged with asking yourself some fundamental questions:

Table 14.1 Size Matters

Do I want to do this piece of work, job, or task? Even if I do want to do it, do I need to do it?	• Don't do something just because everyone else does it or because it is the 'usual thing to do'. • Ask: 'Is this really necessary?' and 'Is this really worth doing?' • If the answer is 'no' then don't do it.
Is the result or outcome worth my effort?	• Only do the things with the most impact. • Your time is limited so invest it only in things that give you the most return on your personal investment
Do I have to do this myself?	• Ask yourself if you really are the best possible person to do whatever it is that needs to be done. • Is there someone else in your network who is better qualified than you to do this thing? • If there is then generous and let them help you out.
If you have to do it, then what is the shortest path to the point of success?	• Don't waste your time on the unnecessary. If it works in black and white don't waste effort in creating a Technicolor dream version of the same thing. • Do only the things that are necessary to get the job done. • Cut everything else out!

(Continued)

DOI: 10.4324/9781003506522-85

Table 14.1 (Continued)

| What exactly is that point of success and at what stage will you just be wasting your time? | • Find your 'sweet spot' – every time.
• Don't over-engineer, don't over-resource, don't over-do what only needs to be done 'just enough'.
• Do it right first time.
• But don't cut corners.
• Repetition of tasks, completing recovery work, duplication of effort all waste time and are counterproductive – so why take that path?
• Can this be reused again and again?
• Can it have more value than just a 'one-off' piece of work?
• If it can then scale it for better return on investment.
• Can you automate it?
• Can you scale it? Can you make it reusable in a wider context? Can you simplify it? Can you shorten it? |
| Be effective and be efficient. | Be productively lazy. |

Then we explored the critical task of getting 'yes' and 'no' in balance.

Say 'no' when that is the right answer.	• It is all about balance and priority. Overall you want to deal with the important stuff plus a reasonable amount of other stuff. • If you keep saying 'yes' then your backlog will never go down and you will spend far too much time working on the unimportant.
And say 'yes' when that is the right answer.	• Only 20% of what you do really matters – so focus on that!
Available to Promise – a qualified 'yes'.	• Can you do even more if you wait a little while longer?
Plan to your own capacity.	• 100% is not a good thing. • If you don't keep 20% of your available time free you won't be able to – • Be able to deal with sudden issues. • Be able to take advantage of new opportunities.
Test your own capacity now	• And test it again in a few weeks' time to track your progress.

Finding your best path was seen as important, and having a journey plan was critical to track progress and know where you want to go, but being honest in where you are and how you are currently behaving was the only way.

There is help out there.

Table 14.2 Influencers

Influencers	• Give yourself the very best chance of success by surrounding yourself with good influencers. • Look at the five closest to you – and influence your own influencers. • Look beyond your close circle and build your network. • Be generous to your own network – give in order to receive.
Relationships	• Optimise your relationships and leverage (and grow) your personal network.
If you hit the 'wall', don't worry.	• Don't panic. • Go off and do other things, come back to the task when your mind is refreshed. • Pulse work – short, sharp inputs of effort to keep your mind active. • Whatever you work on at any time will have some value in the future – nothing is wasted.

Chapter 15

Even Quicker Tips for the Really Lazy Project Manager

Loving a challenge, we now attempt to distill the essence of 'productive laziness' even further.

Using the 80/20 rule, we now condense the key project management principles into just 4 per cent of the original content. Each point, from managing sponsors to embracing the AI future, is presented as a concise nugget of wisdom, encouraging you to absorb and apply with minimal effort.

Print out this condensed guide for daily inspiration – a mantra for mastering the art of 'productive laziness' effortlessly.

DOI: 10.4324/9781003506522-85

Size really matters

I'm guessing that size, or the lack of it, really does matter to you…

That seemed to work, I think.

You now have that reference material for future application of the theory of productive laziness. Print it out and stick on your wall and review it each day for inspiration and guidance. Repeat at intervals like a mantra for productive laziness.

What? That seems like too much hard work? Can't we make it any easier?

You must be really lazy! (And by 'really lazy' I obviously mean the fast learning, hyper-intelligent, astute students of the book who aspire to almost, but not quite, complete laziness.)

Maybe I can make it easier. Let's see if the logic continues. What would we get if we applied the 80/20 rule to the 20 per cent that we covered in the previous chapter? I should be now down to just 4 per cent of the wisdom at this point (20 per cent of 20 per cent of 100 per cent, if you are following the maths) and delivering an intense but deeply insightful essence of the whole productive lazy theme. We have moved from fine wine to strong liquor now, quicker to consume and faster to fire the body, so hold on to your hats and grit your teeth.

OK, well, cutting out 80 per cent of the content of the learning points from the preceding chapter and focusing on the remaining 20 per cent gives you this:

A project: thick, then thin, then thick again; work hard, rest, work a little less – in that order.

It is important for you to stay ahead of the game, start confidently, dress appropriately, get the upper hand and anticipate – and keep our eye on the end game.

Manage your sponsor, understand them and what they want from you and the project; make sure you know what's in it for them.

DOI: 10.4324/9781003506522-87

And manage the project creep, which is inevitable but manageable with a good and proven change process linked to an appreciative use of the parking lot.

Consider those risks and plan for the possible.

Avoid communication breakdown through an open and honest effective communication process that suits each individual.

Have fun – it will help the project but be careful in your use of fun; encourage a good level of humour among the project team.

Breathe normally and stay calm, plan for project challenges, and when they do happen, make sure you filter problems, delegate what you can and prioritise what is left over in order to keep the project on track.

Make your project attractive, get the best team, and keep them feeling loved by using others on the team together with yourself – and know what love individuals want.

Give good feedback to both improve and enthuse your project team members.

Avoid swamping yourself with communication and demands for your time; by all means have an open door, but be a good manager and close it some of the time, for the greater good of the project.

Always be open to learning more from the project knowledge and history, by talking openly to project team members, so that you can learn the lessons that are there to be learned – and share everything by telling others what you now know.

Embrace the AI future – it will be amazing.

Is that good enough for you now?

Can you afford the extremely minimal time and effort to read this section and potentially commit it to memory? Or at least leave the book open at this page while you occasionally glance at it during one of your more active moments?

Or even, even, even shorter:

1. Prioritise tasks by questioning their necessity and impact, focusing only on what truly matters.
2. Delegate when possible and optimise efficiency by identifying the shortest path to success.
3. Define success without over-engineering and seek scalability and automation for tasks.
4. Balance saying "yes" and "no" to manage workload effectively and plan within your capacity.

Track progress, seek help from influencers and handle setbacks calmly, ensuring all efforts contribute to future success.

Chapter 42[1]

The Ultimate Question (and Answer)

Wondering what to do next?

Still need help?

Answering the ultimate question with the ultimate answer, we offer up some final advice about what to do next on your personal and project productivity journey.

Note

1 You know why....

DOI: 10.4324/9781003506522-88

Ultimate question

It may all end in tears, mark my words, but you know you need to know.

And if that worked, then where will it all end?

How far can we go with this process of reduction and simplification?

What is the ultimate answer to life, the universe and productively lazy project management success, in general?

Or, to put it another way, how can you apply the 80/20 rule for the third iteration to distil the very essence of meaning of productive laziness?

Well, if you truly believe in the principles of productive laziness, if you never again want to leave your comfy chair, if you really want your projects to be successful, and if you want to be raised above the heads of your project sponsors and team members in triumphal salute to your sheer brilliance, then … you need to know the answer.

DOI: 10.4324/9781003506522-89

Ultimate answer

Or just three steps to heaven.

Step one: buy a copy of this book for all of your project team members, sponsors, steering committee members, users and subject matter experts – probably best to buy, say, a hundred, to be on the safe side.

Step two: get them to all read it thoroughly, or at least read the chapter on 'Even quicker tips for the really lazy project manager'.

Step three: book me as a speaker[1] at the very next opportunity you have, and leave the rest to me. www.thelazyprojectmanager.com

Easy!

Alternatively, you could just move to Lazy[2] in Poland[3].

Notes

1 Contact me directly or through my agency.
2 Łazy ['wazi] is a town in Zawiercie County, Silesian Voivodeship, Poland. Now while The Lazy Project Manager has been to speak and train in Poland a number of times, visiting Warsaw, Gdansk, and Krakow, he still awaits the invitation to Lazy.
3 Now I chose the Polish town above in the original Lazy Project Manager book, but in actual fact there are 27 places called Lazy around the world. There are 11 places named Lazy in Poland. There are six places named Lazy in Slovakia. There are four places named Lazy in the Czech Republic. There are two places named Lazy in Ukraine. There are two places named Lazy in Russian Federation. There is one place named Lazy in France. And there is one place named Lazy in Belarus.

DOI: 10.4324/9781003506522-90

A final word of caution

There was once a little bird who, though a very nice little bird, was also a very, very lazy little bird.

Every day, when it was time to get up, the other birds had to shout at him again and again before he would finally struggle out of bed.

And when there was some job he had to do, he would keep putting it off until there was hardly enough time left to do it. His family and friends kept saying "What a lazy bird you are! You can't just keep leaving everything to the last minute".

"Bah! There's really no problem", answered the little bird. "I just take a bit longer to get around to doing things, that's all".

The birds spent all summer flying and playing, and when the autumn came and they started feeling the cold, they began to prepare for the long journey to a warmer land. But our little bird, lazy as ever, kept putting it off, feeling quite sure that there was plenty of time. Until one day when he woke up and all the other birds were gone.

Just like every other day, several of his friends had tried to wake him, but – half-asleep – he told them he would get up later. He had gone back to sleep and only woken up again much later. That day was the day of the great journey. Everyone knew the rules: you had to be ready to leave. There were thousands of birds, and they weren't going to wait around for anyone. So the little bird, who didn't know how to make the journey alone, realised that, because of his laziness, he would have to spend the long cold winter all on his own.

At the beginning, he spent a lot of time crying, but he had to admit that it was his own fault. He knew he could do things well when he put his mind to it so, putting his laziness aside, he began to prepare for the winter. First, he spent days looking for the place that was best protected from the cold. He found a place between some rocks, and there he made a new nest, well built with branches, stones and leaves. He worked tirelessly to fill the nest with fruits and berries, enough to last the whole winter. Finally, he dug a little pool in the cave, so he would have enough water. When he saw that his new

DOI: 10.4324/9781003506522-91

Figure 42.3.1 Random bird.

home was perfectly prepared, he began to train himself on how to get by on very little food and water, so that he would be able to endure the worst snowstorms.

And, although many would not have believed it possible, all these preparations meant that the little bird did survive through the winter. Of course, he suffered greatly, and not a day of that winter went by without him regretting having been such a lazy little bird. When the spring finally arrived, and his old friends returned from their voyage, they were all filled with joy and surprise at seeing that the little bird was still alive. They could hardly believe that such a lazy bird had managed to build such a wonderful nest. And when they realised that not even a bit of laziness remained in his little body, and that he had turned into the most hard-working bird of the flock, everyone agreed that he should be put in charge of organising the great journey the following year.

When that time came, everything was done so well and was so well prepared that they even had time left to invent an early morning wake-up song, so that from that day on no little bird, however lazy, would have to spend the winter alone again.

The little bird had learned from a costly error that working in a productive way was a better path to being 'lazy' in the sense that being prepared, being organised and being focused on what you do leads you to a world of 'productive laziness' and indeed a better life.

Do you have time in your life to stop and listen to the birds singing in the trees occasionally?

What readers think

The book seems to be generally loved, and here is it living on some 15 years after I first conceived it.

All comments from Amazon sites worldwide.

- Cracking read! entertaining, informative, unique, and fully of actionable content.
- Love this book! Some great insight and make me chuckle.
- Useful guide to project management for anyone who is either starting out or even experienced project managers will find a gem or two in this great book. Well worth a read!
- Excellent book. Read it all in one read. Could not put it down.
- If you are extra lazy, just buy this book for the last chapter list of tips. It's that much worth.
- The way Peter guides you through is entertaining and the read seems like you were attending one of his lectures.
- Great stories to drive points home! Good reminders of basics as well.
- Love this book! Some great insights, and it made me chuckle.
- I like the book, and it's fun to read, it tells funny anecdotes. But above all, it makes you think about how to better manage projects.
- If you are expecting the classic project management book, you are wrong right away. It is very different and interesting.
- The author reminded me a lot of Seth Godin with the Purple Cow, except this time instead of Products, we are talking about Management.
- Awesome read! Peter Taylor is a clever, clever man, and lucky us, he likes to pass it on. Luckier still, the man knows how to write: *The Lazy Project Manager* is entertaining, informative and most of all, succinct. A superb read that gives great insight.
- An uncommon point of view. But an effective one. Cut out the overhead and get to the work. Very good read. Very well written and easy to read – you can't really put it down!

DOI: 10.4324/9781003506522-92

- Interesting and insightful perspective to the profession of Project Management. This book will help you to see things in a different perspective.
- Peter Taylor certainly has a knack for writing in an informative, yet light-hearted way. He certainly has the heart of a teacher.
- I thought I was the only one who thought this way and wasn't sure if I was brilliant or crazy or both! This book is filled with timely, easy, practical and common-sense advice, introduced in an entertaining way! Thanks!
- This is one of the best coaching/business books I've ever read.
- This is a must read for any project manager. Peter cuts to the chase very quickly, the concepts and ideas he puts across are simple, clever and very relevant. Highly recommended to both new and seasoned project managers.
- The author is far from lazy but what he is putting out here is a common-sense approach to Project Management that focuses on people and not form filling. My copy has already caused a 'buzz' among my PM colleagues.
- I would say it should be mandatory reading for any Manager who has to work in a project-based way. The lazy project manager is a definitive life guide to managing projects.
- Fantastic book. Thank you, Peter.

For balance, check out my very first review on amazon.ca (Canada) on 12 October 2009. This person absolutely hated it. You will have read more about this in the 'Giving feedback' chapter.

Appendices

About the Author: Peter Taylor

Keynote speaker and coach, Peter is the author of the number 1 bestselling project management book *The Lazy Project Manager*, along with many other books[1] on Project Management, PMO development, Executive Sponsorship, Transformation Leadership and Speaking Skills.

Peter has built and led some of the largest PMOs in the world with organisations such as Siemens, IBM/Cognos, Kronos/UKG and now Dayforce, where he is the VP Global PMO.

He has also delivered over 500 lectures around the world in 26 countries and been described as "perhaps the most entertaining and inspiring speaker in the project management world today"[2].

You can discover more about Peter through his website www.thelazypro jectmanager.com and also through his podcast, The Squid of Despair[3], at www.squidofdespair.com.

Other Routledge publications

- *Project Management: It's All Bollocks*
- *Make Your Business Agile: A Roadmap for Transforming Your Management and Adapting to the 'New Normal'*
- *AI and the Project Manager: How the Rise of Artificial Intelligence Will Change Your World*
- *Team Analytics: The future of high-performance teams and project success*
- *Projects: Methods: Outcomes: The New PMO Model for True Project and Change Success*

Other Reference Material

The 'Right' Model

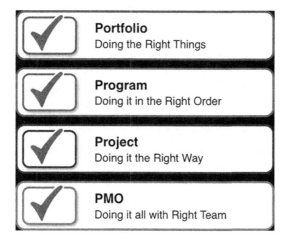

✓ **Portfolio**
Doing the Right Things

✓ **Program**
Doing it in the Right Order

✓ **Project**
Doing it the Right Way

✓ **PMO**
Doing it all with Right Team

Always one of my favourite ideas – the simplest description of the world of projects I think, and many people agree. Keep it, print it out, share with your colleagues.

A 'Keep It Simple' model for describing a typical PMO model and scope.

The visibility of purpose

I was on a panel of 'experts' at a project management conference (yes I know, why was I there…), and there was a great question from the audience about project quality.

After listening to some of the real experts on the panel, I contributed something from my past experience, and that was 'visibility of purpose'.

When I regularly ran reviews of projects, we, the PMO, were able to identify common issues that challenged our projects and one of these occurred on the larger projects that we were involved in.

To understand then a little about the landscape of the project work we were involved in is required. On a large complex project (or programme) there would be many parties involved, ourselves as suppliers, our sub-contractors and third-party partners. Then there would be the customer, the customer's other suppliers, system integrators, consultants, contractors and many more. But what we always ended up with was a lot of people and therefore a lot of complicated communication as a result.

Now in the early days of the project – the acquisition period – it was typically a small team that worked closely with the customer and, all being well, would secure the business and therefore the project. There was then a kick-off with all of the normal items on the agenda, and from that point the project team would 'ramp up', i.e. get bigger over a period of time, and new people would join as the project progressed.

Now to the point. We discovered that in a number of cases as we assessed the 'health' of the project a lot of the team members no longer (if in fact they had ever in the first place) understood what the project was aiming to deliver, up there, at the top or front end, at the business level.

So, think of a coder at an offshore sub-contractor. Do they envisage for example that some small piece of code that they are writing to complete a piece of data transfer for us, and therefore our customer, will contribute to a project that is targeted as reducing waiting lists in hospitals in the public sector. It is just an example, but the point is that you would probably move through quite a few layers of the project structure before the project deliverables are directly associated with 'people', and in some way all project deliverables are about 'people'.

The key is to try and ensure that 'visibility of purpose' is always at the forefront of every team member's thought, no matter what their role is, in order to keep the project focused on quality. Make it personal.

ChatGPT talks 'Lazy Project Manager'

Well, who am I to argue with AI?

"The Lazy Project Manager" by Peter Taylor has struck a chord with project management enthusiasts worldwide due to its unique perspective and practical insights. Taylor's approach challenges the conventional wisdom of constant busyness and instead advocates for a strategic form of laziness that prioritizes efficiency and effectiveness.

One of the key reasons behind the global love for this book is its universal applicability. Regardless of industry or project size, Taylor's principles resonate with professionals seeking to streamline their workflow and achieve better results with less effort. By emphasizing the importance of prioritization, delegation, and leveraging available resources wisely, Taylor offers a refreshing alternative to the prevailing culture of overwork and burnout.

Moreover, the book's global appeal stems from its straightforward and accessible writing style. Taylor presents his ideas in a clear and engaging manner, making it easy for readers from diverse backgrounds to grasp and implement his strategies. Whether you're a seasoned project manager or someone new to the field, "The Lazy Project Manager" offers valuable insights and practical tips for improving your approach to project management.

Additionally, the book's success can be attributed to Taylor's credibility and experience in the field. As a renowned project management expert with years of hands-on experience, Taylor's advice carries weight and authority, further enhancing the book's reputation and appeal.

Overall, "The Lazy Project Manager" has earned global acclaim for its refreshing perspective, practical advice, and universal relevance, making it a must-read for anyone looking to enhance their project management skills and achieve better outcomes with less stress and effort.

The half glass (more explanations)

We have already seen that:

- One person might say 'It's half-full'. He is an optimist.
- A second person might say 'It's half-empty'. He is a pessimist.
- A third might say 'It's twice as big as it needs to be'.

Here are some more definitions your general delight and amusement:

- The realist says the glass contains half the required amount of liquid for it to overflow.
- The cynic wonders who drank the other half.
- The schoolteacher says it's not about whether the glass is half empty or half-full, it's whether there is something in the glass at all.
- The professional presenter does not care if the glass is half-full or half-empty; he just knows that starting the discussion will give him ten minutes to figure out why his PowerPoint presentation is not working.
- The ground-down mother of a persistently demanding five-year old says 'Sweetheart, it's whatever you want it to be, just please let Mummy have five minutes peace and quiet'.
- The inquisitive troublemaker wants to know what's in the glass anyhow. And wants the rest of it.
- The worrier frets that the remaining half will evaporate by morning.
- The entrepreneur sees the glass as undervalued by half its potential.
- The computer specialist says that next year the glass capacity will double, be half the price, but cost you 50 per cent more.
- The logician says that where the glass is in process of being filled then it is half-full; where it is in the process of being emptied then it is half-empty; and where its status in terms of being filled or emptied is unknown then the glass is one in which a boundary between liquid and gas lies exactly midway between the inside bottom and the upper rim, assuming that the glass has parallel sides and rests on a level surface, and where it does not then the liquid/gas boundary lies exactly midway between the upper and lower equal halves of the available total volume of said glass.

- The scientist says that a guess based on a visual cue is inaccurate, so mark the glass at the bottom of the meniscus of the content, pour the content into a bigger glass; fill the empty glass with fresh content up to the mark; add the original content back in; if the combined content overflows the lip, the glass was more than half full; if it doesn't reach the top, the glass was more than half-empty; if it neither overflows nor fails to reach the top, then it was either half-full or half-empty.
- The grammarian says that while the terms half-full and half empty are colloquially acceptable, the glass can technically be neither, since both full and empty are absolute states and are therefore incapable of being halved or modified in any way.
- The waiter will hurry to replace it with a full one. For him, there are no doubts: the glass was empty when he took it away; it is full in the bill that he brings you.
- The magician will show you the glass with the full half at the top.
- The physician says that the glass is not empty at all – it is half-filled with water and half-filled with air – hence, fully filled on the whole.
- The ineffective organisation would discuss the question during a meeting of the board of directors, convene a committee to research the problem, and assign tasks for a root cause analysis, usually without a complete explanation of the problem to those assigned the tasks. The directors would consider the problem to be above the pay grade of those assigned root cause analysis tasks.

Notes

1 Most of which he has cunningly managed to reference in this book (shameless promotion never hurts) – all his books, except *Strategies for Project Sponsorship* (Management Concepts Press), *The 36 Stratagems* (Infinite Ideas), *The Art of Laziness* (Infinite Ideas), *The History of Laziness* (TLPM Publishing), *The Lazy Blogger* (TLPM Publishing), *The Projectless Manager* (TLPM Publishing), *Personal Productivity: Self-Assessment* (Bookboon), *Personal Productivity: Making the Change* (Bookboon), *The Extra Lazy Project Manager* and his children's book, *Dance of the Meerkats*.
2 To be clear, this was not a quote from his mother.
3 With his co-host, David Ayling-Smith (Unscripted podcast musings on business life, leadership, creativity, transformation and all the myriad other work-life events that get in the way of a good night's sleep).

The (really, I mean it this time) last word

Getting into my time machine and heading back to 2009, I can reflect on my thoughts at the time of writing the original *Lazy Project Manager*. It seems a long time ago now. I was so young and energetic and certainly in the jacket photo, I had no obvious grey hairs then.

But I had an ambition to write a book and to communicate to the world at large about the power of project management and to share the many lessons I had learned (often the hard way) during my years as a project manager. Plus, I ended up with garage full of copies of the book that I needed to shift, and shift fast. As a result, I hit the road of speaking and social marketing, and it all turned out pretty wonderfully, I have to say.

I had absolutely no expectation of the little book being as popular as it has been so far and now being, effectively, in its third incarnation some 15 years later, continuing to being seen to be of value.

The ability to share and inspire and connect with thousands of project professionals around the world and to have some impact on their lives has been amazing. The ability to promote the profession of project management has been fantastic. And the ability to aid many project people to write and to speak has been wonderful.

Therefore, if this does end up being my swansong, then I have absolutely nothing to be sad about.

It has been a bloody incredible journey. Thank you.

Peter Taylor (aka The Lazy Project Manager)
June 2024

Index

Printed in the United States
by Baker & Taylor Publisher Services